# Table of Contents

# Mental Arithmetic
## 2× through 5×

Score

11 /11 ✓

**1** Multiply.

(1) $2 \times 1 = 2$ ✓

(2) $2 \times 3 = 6$ ✓

(3) $2 \times 7 = 14$ ✓

(4) $3 \times 4 = 12$ ✓

(5) $3 \times 8 = 24$ ✓

(6) $4 \times 2 = 8$ ✓

(7) $4 \times 5 = 20$ ✓

(8) $4 \times 9 = 36$ ✓

(9) $5 \times 3 = 15$ ✓

(10) $5 \times 6 = 30$ ✓

**2** If a loaf of bread is $3, how much will 7 loaves of bread cost?

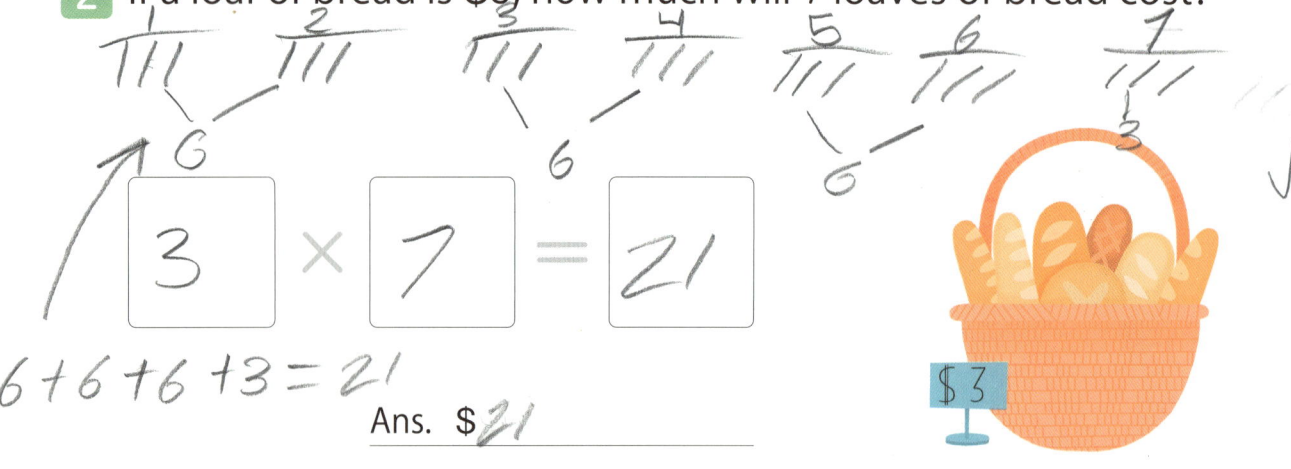

$3 \times 7 = 21$

$6 + 6 + 6 + 3 = 21$

Ans. $21

**Check your answers. If you missed any problems, pick one to retry.**

$\times$    =

Name  Date 6 / 12 / 24

Score 11 / 11

**1** Multiply.

(1) $6 \times 2 = 12$ ✓

(2) $6 \times 8 = 48$ ✓

(3) $7 \times 1 = 7$ ✓

(4) $7 \times 5 = 35$ ✓

(5) $8 \times 3 = 24$ ✓

(6) $8 \times 7 = 56$ ✓

(7) $9 \times 4 = 36$ ✓

(8) $9 \times 9 = 81$ ✓

(9) $1 \times 6 = 6$ ✓

(10) $1 \times 8 = 8$ ✓

**2** There are 8 peaches in a box. How many peaches are in 6 boxes?

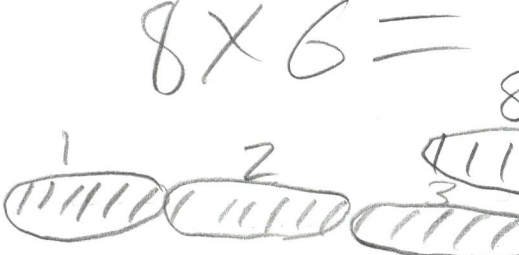

$8 \times 6 =$ ✓

Ans. 48 peaches

 **Check your answers. If you missed any problems, pick one to retry.**

Name _Renee_  Date _6 / 12 / 24_

Score _11_ / _11_

**1** Multiply.

(1) $1 \times 10 = 10$  ✓

(2) $2 \times 10 = 20$  ✓

(3) $4 \times 10 = 40$  ✓

(4) $7 \times 10 = 70$  ✓

(5) $9 \times 10 = 90$  ✓

(6) $3 \times 11 = 33$  ✓

(7) $6 \times 11 = 66$  ✓

(8) $8 \times 11 = 88$  ✓

(9) $1 \times 12 = 12$  ✓

(10) $5 \times 12 = 60$  ✓

**2** There are 5 boxes of apples. Each box holds 11 apples. How many apples are there in total?

✓

$11 \times 5 = $   $5 \times 11 = 55$

I dont like the equation 11×5, so i flipped it around and counted by fives to get the answer.

Ans. _55_ apples

**Check your answers. If you missed any problems, pick one to retry.**

4

Name Reneé

Date 6 /13/ 24

Score II / 11

**1** Multiply.

(1) $10 \times 1 = 10$ ✓

(2) $10 \times 3 = 30$ ✓

(3) $11 \times 2 = 22$ ✓

(4) $11 \times 6 = 66$ ✓

(5) $12 \times 1 = 12$ ✓

(6) $12 \times 5 = 60$ ✓

(7) $0 \times 4 = 0$ ✓

(8) $0 \times 8 = 0$ ✓

(9) $7 \times 0 = 0$ ✓

(10) $9 \times 0 = 0$ ✓

**2** Maya bought 4 packages of eggs. Each package contains 12 eggs. How many eggs did she buy in all?

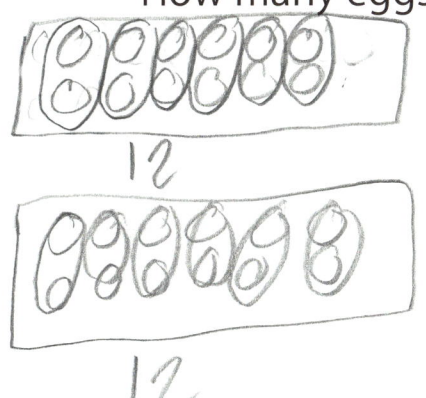
12

12

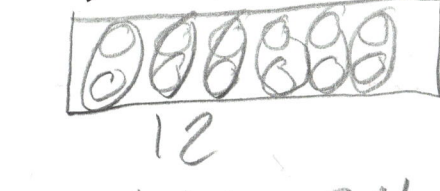
12

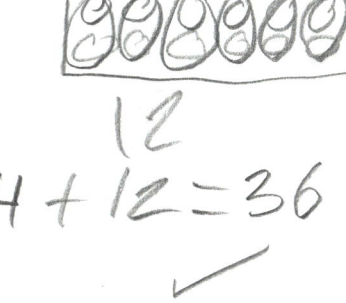
12

$12 + 12 = 24$   $24 + 12 = 36$
$36 + 12 = \textcircled{48}$

Ans. 48 eggs

 Check & Fix

**Check your answers. If you missed any problems, pick one to retry.**

5

Name

Date 6 /13/ 24

Score 11 /11

## 1 Multiply.

(1) $20 \times 3 = 60$ ✓

(2) $30 \times 5 = 150$ ✓

(3) $50 \times 9 = 450$ ✓

(4) $60 \times 2 = 120$ ✓

(5) $90 \times 8 = 720$ ✓

(6) $100 \times 6 = 600$ ✓

(7) $200 \times 1 = 200$

(8) $400 \times 2 = 800$ ✓

(9) $700 \times 7 = 4900$ ✓

(10) $800 \times 4 = 3200$ ✓

## 2 Each package of "Thank You" cards has 60 cards. How many cards are in 3 packages?

$$60 \times 2 = 120$$
$$120 + 60 = 180$$

Ans. 180 ✓ cards

**Check your answers. If you missed any problems, pick one to retry.**

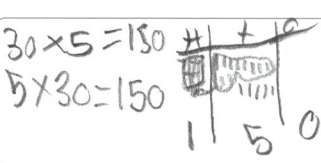

$30 \times 5 = 150$
$5 \times 30 = 150$

6

# 6 Mental Arithmetic
## Mixed ①

Name _ReneL_  Date _6/13/24_

Score _11/11_

**I** Multiply.

(1) $2 \times 3 = 6$ ✓

(2) $5 \times 9 = 45$ ✓

(3) $8 \times 5 = 40$ ✓

(4) $1 \times 7 = 7$ ✓

(5) $3 \times 11 = 33$ ✓

(6) $7 \times 10 = 70$ ✓

(7) $12 \times 2 = 24$ ✓

(8) $0 \times 8 = 0$ ✓

(9) $40 \times 3 = 120$ ✓

(10) $600 \times 4 = 2400$ ✓

**2** There are 9 tables, and 5 students can sit at each table. How many students can sit in total?

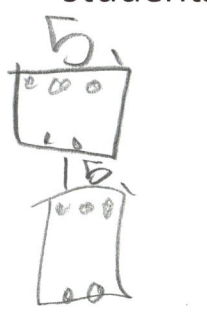    

$5 \times 9 = 45$ ✓

Ans. _45_ students

 **Check your answers. If you missed any problems, pick one to retry.**

Name Renie

Date 6/14/24

Score 1 /11

## 1 Multiply.

(1)  $4 \times 7 = 28$

(6)  $1 \times 12 = 12$

(2)  $3 \times 4 = 12$

(7)  $10 \times 5 = 50$

(3)  $9 \times 2 = 18$

(8)  $6 \times 0 = 0$

(4)  $7 \times 8 = 56$

(9)  $90 \times 1 = 90$

(5)  $5 \times 10 = 50$

(10)  $300 \times 9 = 2700$

## 2 If Cora makes 20 candles and sells each candle for $8, how much money can she make?

$8 \times 20 = 160$

$2 \times 8 = 160$

1 6 0

Ans. $ 160

**Check your answers.**
**If you missed any**
**problems, pick one**
**to retry.**

# 8 Column Multiplication ①
## 2 Digit × 1 Digit ①

**1** Multiply.

(1)
```
      1 2
  ×     3
②3×1  3 6  ①3×2
```
←

(2)
```
      3 1
  ×     3
      9 3
```
←

(3)
```
      4 2
  ×     2
      8 4
```
←

**2** Rewrite the problem vertically. Then multiply.

(1) 22 × 4
```
      2 2
  ×     4
      8 8
```

(2) 11 × 8
```
      1 1
  ×     8
      8 8
```

**3** A case of soda has 12 cans. How many cans of soda are in 4 cases?

12 × 4 =

```
      1 2
  ×     4
      4 8
```

Ans. 48 cans

Check your answers. If you missed any problems, pick one to retry.

Check & Fix

Name _Reatie_  Date 6 /14 /24

Score 6 / 6

**1** Multiply.

> ① 2 × 6 = 12
> 2 is in the ones place, and 1 is carried over to the tens place.

(1)
```
    3 6
  ×   2
  ─────
  7 2
```

> ② 2 × 3 = 6
> 7 is in the tens place, as 6 + the carried over 1.

(2)
```
    2 7
  ×   3
  ─────
    8 1
```

(3)
```
    1 8
  ×   5
  ─────
    9 0
```

**2** Rewrite the problem vertically. Then multiply.

(1) 29 × 3
```
    2 9
  ×   3
  ─────
    8 7
```

(2) 16 × 5
```
    1 6
  ×   5
  ─────
    8 0
```

**3** If a carton of strawberries has 24 strawberries, how many strawberries are in 4 cartons?

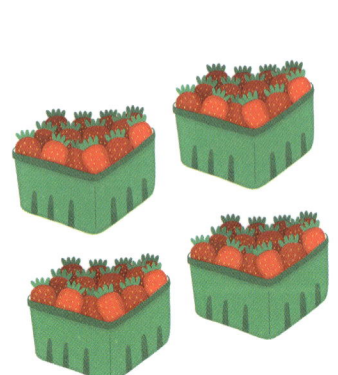

```
      2 4
        4
  ×
  ───────
      1 6
  +   8
  ───────
      9 6
```

Ans. _96_ strawberries

> Check your answers. If you missed any problems, pick one to retry.
>
> **Check & Fix**

Name _Rmee_

Date _6/15/24_

Score _6_ / 6

**1** Multiply.

(1)
```
        3 2
      ×   4
```
② 4 × 3    **128**    ① 4 × 2

(2)
```
        6 4
      ×   2
      ─────
      1 2 8
```

(3)
```
        8 3
      ×   3
      ─────
      2 4 9
```

**2** Rewrite the problem vertically. Then multiply.

(1) 84 × 2
```
      8 4
   ×   2
   ───────
   1 6 8
```

(2) 52 × 4
```
      5 2
   ×   4
   ───────
   2 0 8
```

**3** A bus can hold 62 students. How many students can 4 buses hold?

```
      6 2
   ×   4
   ───────
   2 4 8
```

246 students can ride in 4 school buses

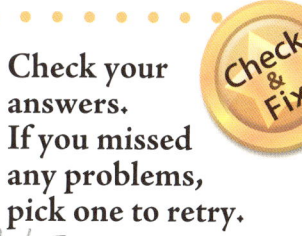

Check your answers.
If you missed any problems, pick one to retry.

Ans. _248_ students

11

Name _Renee_   Date _6/16/24_

Score _6 / 6_

## 1 Multiply.

(1) ✓
```
    40
×    2
```
② 2 × 4   **80**   ① 2 × 0

(2) ✓
```
    60
×    5
   300
```

(3) ✓
```
    70
×    3
   210
```

## 2 Rewrite the problem vertically. Then multiply.

(1) 60 × 9
```
    60
×    9
   540
```

(2) ✓ 30 × 3
```
    30
×    3
    90
```

## 3 If Scott is driving 60 miles per hour, how far can he drive in 4 hours?

✓

60 × 4 = 240

```
    60
×    4
   240
```

honk honk!

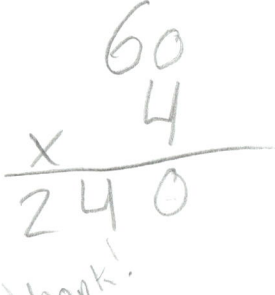

Ans. _240_ miles

Name _mon_ _Renee_♡

Date 6 /17/24

Score **6** / 6

**1** Multiply.

> ① 3 × 6 = 18
> 8 is in the ones place, and 1 is carried over to the tens place.

(1)
$$\begin{array}{r} {}^{+1}76 \\ \times \quad 3 \\ \hline \boxed{2}2\boxed{8} \end{array}$$

> ② 3 × 7 = 21
> 2 is in the tens place, as 1 + the carried over 1.

(2)
$$\begin{array}{r} 24 \\ \times \quad 6 \\ \hline 1\;44 \end{array}$$

(3)
$$\begin{array}{r} 72 \\ \times \quad 6 \\ \hline 4\;32 \end{array}$$

**2** Rewrite the problem vertically. Then multiply.

(1) 64 × 7

$$\begin{array}{r} 64 \\ \times \quad 7 \\ \hline 448 \end{array}$$

(2) 46 × 5

$$\begin{array}{r} 46 \\ \times \quad 5 \\ \hline 230 \end{array}$$

**3** Paul makes $25 mowing a lawn. How much will he make if he mows 6 lawns?

25 × 6 =

$$\begin{array}{r} 25 \\ \times \quad 6 \\ \hline 150 \end{array}$$

Paul can make $25 dollars if he mows 6 lawns.

Check your answers. If you missed any problems, pick one to retry.

**Check & Fix**

Ans. $ 150

13

**Column Multiplication ①**
2 Digit × 1 Digit ⑥

Name **Renée**

Date **6 /17 /24**

Score **6 / 6**

**1** Multiply.

> ① $3 × 7 = 21$
> 1 is in the ones place, and 2 is carried over to the tens place.

(1)
```
    3 7
  ×   3
  -----
  1 1 1
```

> ② $3 × 3 = 9$
> 1 is in the tens place, as $9 +$ the carried over 2.

(2)
```
    1 6
  ×   8
  -----
  1 2 8
```

(3)
```
    2 5
  ×   4
  -----
  1 0 0
```

**2** Rewrite the problem vertically. Then multiply.

(1) $29 × 4$
```
    2 9
  ×   4
  -----
  1 3 6
```

(2) $39 × 3$
```
    3 9
  ×   3
  -----
  1 1 7
```

**3** Kathy has 3 bags with 35 buttons in each bag. How many buttons does she have altogether?

$35 × 3 = 105$

```
    3 5
  ×   3
  -----
  1 0 5
```

Ans. **105** buttons

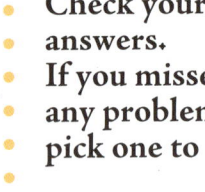

Check your answers. If you missed any problems, pick one to retry.

Check & Fix

14

# 14 Column Multiplication ①
## 2 Digit × 1 Digit ⑦

## 1 Multiply.

(1)
```
    6 9
  ×   3
  ² 
  2 0 7
```

(2)
```
    8 4
  ×   6
  ² 
  5 0 4
```
(5 6 4)

(3)
```
    7 7
  ×   4
  3 0 8
```
(3 8 8)

## 2 Rewrite the problem vertically. Then multiply.

(1) 38 × 9
```
    3 8
  ×   9
  3 ⁷ 2
```
(3 4 2)

(2) 87 × 7
```
    8 7
  ×   7
  6 ⁴ 9
```
(6 0 9)

## 3 There are 24 desks in a classroom. How many desks are in 9 classrooms?

```
    2 4
  ×   9
  2 ³ 6
```
(2 1 6)

Check your answers.
If you missed any problems, pick one to retry.

**Check & Fix**

Ans. __216__ desks

15

# 15 Column Multiplication ①
## 2 Digit × 1 Digit ⑧

Name *Renee*

Date 6/18/24

Score 4/6

## 1 Multiply.

(1)
$$\begin{array}{r} 21 \\ \times\ 4 \\ \hline 84 \end{array}$$

(2)
$$\begin{array}{r} 41 \\ \times\ 8 \\ \hline 32\,8 \end{array}$$

(3)
$$\begin{array}{r} 53 \\ \times\ 9 \\ \hline 4\,57 \end{array}$$

## 2 Rewrite the problem vertically. Then multiply.

(1) 80 × 5
$$\begin{array}{r} 80 \\ \times\ 5 \\ \hline 400 \end{array}$$

(2) 27 × 8
$$\begin{array}{r} 27 \\ \times\ 8 \\ \hline 216 \end{array}$$

## 3 A parking lot has 16 rows and there are 7 cars in each row. How many cars are in the parking lot altogether?

$7 \times 16 = 112$

$$\begin{array}{r} 16 \\ \times\ 7 \\ \hline 112 \end{array}$$

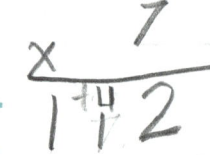

Ans. 112 cars

Check your answers. If you missed any problems, pick one to retry.

Check & Fix

16

Tue

# Column Multiplication ①
## 2 Digit × 1 Digit ⑨

Name _kmee_  Date 6/19/24

Score C/6

## ☐ Multiply.

(1)

$$
\begin{array}{r}
39 \\
\times\ 2 \\
\hline
78
\end{array}
$$

✓ (2)

$$
\begin{array}{r}
80 \\
\times\ 6 \\
\hline
480
\end{array}
$$

✓ (3)

$$
\begin{array}{r}
38 \\
\times\ 6 \\
\hline
228
\end{array}
$$

## 2 Rewrite the problem vertically. Then multiply.

✓ (1) 43 × 2

$$
\begin{array}{r}
43 \\
\times\ 2 \\
\hline
86
\end{array}
$$

✓ (2) 17 × 6

$$
\begin{array}{r}
17 \\
6 \\
\times \\
\hline
102
\end{array}
$$

## 3 If a jacket costs $75, how much would 8 jackets cost?

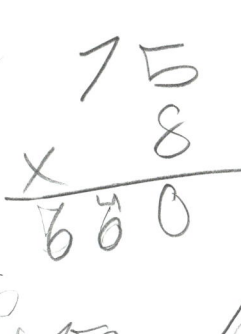

$$
\begin{array}{r}
75 \\
\times\ 8 \\
\hline
600
\end{array}
$$

Ans. $ 600

Check your answers. If you missed any problems, pick one to retry.

Check & Fix

17

Tue

Name
Renee

Date
6/19/24

Score
8 / 8

**1** Multiply.

(1)
```
    3 1 4
  ×     2
    6 2 8
```
③ 2 × 3    ① 2 × 4
② 2 × 1

(3)
```
    4 2 1
  ×     2
    8 4 2
```

(5)
```
    3 2 1
  ×     3
    9 6 3
```

(2)
```
    1 3 2
  ×     3
    3 9 6
```

(4)
```
    1 2 1
  ×     4
    4 8 4
```

(6)
```
    2 4 4
  ×     2
    4 8 8
```

**2** Rewrite the problem vertically. Then multiply.

(1)  2 3 3 × 3
```
    2 3 3
  ×     3
    6 9 9
```

(2)  4 1 3 × 2
```
    4 1 3
  ×     2
    8 2 6
```

18

# Column Multiplication ②
## 3 Digit × 1 Digit ②

Name _____ Date 6 /20/ 24

Score 8 / 8

## 1 Multiply.

(1)
```
    3 4 8
  ×     2
  -------
    6 9 6
```

①2 × 8 = 16
6 is in the ones place, and 1 is carried over to the tens place.

③2 × 3

②2 × 4 = 8
9 is in the tens place, as 8＋ the carried over 1.

(3)
```
    3 1 5
  ×     3
  -------
    9 4 5
```

(5)
```
    4 2 5
  ×     2
  -------
    8 5 0
```

(2)
```
    2 1 6
  ×     4
  -------
    8 6 4
```

(4)
```
    1 2 3
  ×     4
  -------
    4 9 2
```

(6)
```
    3 2 7
  ×     3
  -------
    9 8 1
```

## 2 Rewrite the problem vertically. Then multiply.

(1) 118 × 5
```
    1 1 8
  ×     5
  -------
    5 9 0
```

(2) 247 × 2
```
    2 4 7
  ×     2
  -------
    4 9 4
```

Check your answers.
If you missed any problems, pick one to retry.

Check & Fix

19

# Column Multiplication ②
## 3 Digit × 1 Digit ③

Name RM

Date 6/20/24

Score 8 / 8

## 1 Multiply.

(1) ✓
```
    2 8 3
  ×     3
  ⁺²
  8 4 9
```

(3) ✓
```
    1 6 2
  ×     4
  ⁺²
  6 4 8
```

(5) ✓
```
    1 8 1
  ×     5
  ⁺⁴
  9 0 5
```

(2) ✓
```
    4 9 1
  ×     2
  ⁺¹
  9 8 2
```

(4) ✓
```
    3 7 4
  ×     2
  ⁺¹
  7 4 8
```

(6) ✓
```
    2 4 2
  ×     3
  ⁺¹
  7 2 6
```

## 2 Rewrite the problem vertically. Then multiply.

(1) ✓ 182 × 4
```
  1 8 2
      4
× ⁺³
  7 2 8
```

(2) ✓ 463 × 2
```
  4 6 3
      2
× ⁺¹
  9 2 6
```

Check your answers.
If you missed any problems, pick one to retry.

Check & Fix

# 20 Column Multiplication ②
## 3 Digit × 1 Digit ④

Name _lonée_   Date 6/21/24

Score 6/6

## 1 Multiply.

(1)
```
    367
  ×   2
  ———
    734
```

(2)
```
    157
  ×   5
  ———
    785
```

(3)
```
    238
  ×   4
  ———
    952
```

## 2 Rewrite the problem vertically. Then multiply.

(1) 136 × 5

```
    136
  ×   5
  ———
    680
```

(2) 274 × 3

```
    274
  ×   3
  ———
    822
```

## 3 Michael puts $145 in the bank each month. How much money will he have in 6 months?

if Michael puts $145
in the bank each month
in 6 month there will
be $870 in the bank after
six month

```
    45
  ×  6
  ———
    870
```

Ans. $ 870

Check your answers. If you missed any problems, pick one to retry.

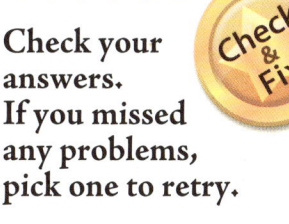

# 21 Column Multiplication ②
## 3 Digit × 1 Digit ⑤

Name _mimes_

Date 6 /21 /24

Score 8 / 8

## 1 Multiply.

(1) ✓
```
    1 2 8
  ×     4
  ─────────
    5 1 2
```

(3) ✓
```
    1 1 8
  ×     7
  ─────────
    8 2 6
```

(5) ✓
```
    1 2 5
  ×     4
  ─────────
    5 0 0
```

(2) ✓
```
    2 3 5
  ×     3
  ─────────
    7 0 5
```

(4) ✓
```
    1 1 6
  ×     7
  ─────────
    8 1 2
```

(6) ✓
```
    2 3 7
  ×     3
  ─────────
    7 1 1
```

## 2 Rewrite the problem vertically. Then multiply.

(1) 226 × 4
```
    2 2 6
  ×     4
  ─────────
    9 0 4
```

(2) 119 × 6
```
    1 1 9
  ×     6
  ─────────
    7 1 4
```

Check your answers. If you missed any problems, pick one to retry.

## 22 Column Multiplication ②
### 3 Digit × 1 Digit ⑥

Name _Renee_  Date 6/22/04

Score 8 / 8

## 1 Multiply.

(1)
```
    320
  ×   3
  ─────
    960
```

(3)
```
    200
  ×   4
  ─────
    800
```

(5)
```
    150
  ×   4
  ─────
    600
```

(2)
```
    430
  ×   2
  ─────
    860
```

(4)
```
    270
  ×   3
  ─────
    810
```

(6)
```
    380
  ×   2
  ─────
    760
```

## 2 Rewrite the problem vertically. Then multiply.

(1) 450 × 2

```
    450
      2
  ×
  ─────
    900
```

(2) 230 × 4

```
    230
      4
  ×
  ─────
    920
```

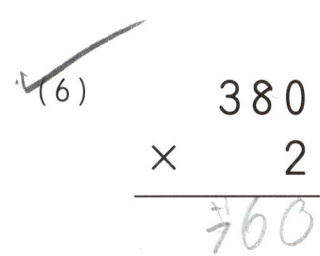

Check your answers. If you missed any problems, pick one to retry.

Check & Fix

23

**23** **Column Multiplication** ②
3 Digit × 1 Digit ⑦

Name Renée

Date 6 /22/24

Score 8 / 8

## 1 Multiply.

(1)
```
    1 0 8
×       4
  ³
  4 3 2
```

(3)
```
    2 0 5
×       3
    ⁺¹
  6 1 5
```

(5)
```
    1 0 6
×       5
      ⁺³
  5 3 0
```

(2)
```
    4 0 7
×       2
    ⁺¹
  8 1 4
```

(4)
```
    3 0 4
×       2
  6 0 8
```

(6)
```
    2 0 9
×       4
    ⁺³
  8 3 6
```

## 2 Rewrite the problem vertically. Then multiply.

(1) 306 × 3

```
  3 0 6
×     3
  ⁺¹
9 1 8
```

(2) 205 × 4

```
  2 0 5
×     4
  ⁺²
8 2 0
```

Check your answers.
If you missed any problems, pick one to retry.

Check & Fix

24

# 24 Column Multiplication ②
## 3 Digit × 1 Digit ⑧

Name _Rmee_ Date 6/23/24

Score 6/6

**1** Multiply.

(1) ✓
```
   321
 ×   4
 1284
```

(2) ✓
```
   643
 ×   2
 1286
```

(3) ✓
```
   411
 ×   5
 2055
```

**2** Rewrite the problem vertically. Then multiply.

(1) ✓ 613 × 3
```
  613
    3
×
1839
```

(2) ✓ 942 × 2
```
  942
    2
×
1884
```

✓

**3** A package of staples has 521 staples. How many staples are in 4 packages?

in 4 pakages of staples in total there are 2084 staples.

```
  521
    4
×
2084
```

STAPLES

Ans. 2084 staples

Check your answers. If you missed any problems, pick one to retry.

Check & Fix

# 25 Column Multiplication ②
## 3 Digit × 1 Digit ⑨

Name *RMÉS*

Date 6 /23/ 24

Score 8 / 8

## 1 Multiply.

(1) ✓
```
    3 1 8
  ×     4
  ───────
  1 2 7 2
```

(3) ✓
```
    2 1 5
  ×     6
  ───────
  1 2 9 0
```

(5) ✓
```
    6 1 4
  ×     5
  ───────
  3 0 7 0
```

(2) ✓
```
    4 2 7
  ×     3
  ───────
  1 2 8 1
```

(4) ✓
```
    7 3 6
  ×     2
  ───────
  1 4 7 2
```

(6) ✓
```
    5 2 9
  ×     3
  ───────
  1 5 8 7
```

## 2 Rewrite the problem vertically. Then multiply.

(1) 816 × 3
```
    8 1 6
  ×     3
  ───────
  2 4 4 8
```

(2) 418 × 5
```
    4 1 8
  ×     5
  ───────
  2 0 9 0
```

Check your answers. If you missed any problems, pick one to retry.

Check & Fix

Name **Renee B** Date 6/24/24

Score **8** / 8

## 1 Multiply.

(1)
$$
\begin{array}{r}
382 \\
\times \quad 4 \\
\hline
1528
\end{array}
$$

(3)
$$
\begin{array}{r}
451 \\
\times \quad 6 \\
\hline
2706
\end{array}
$$

(5)
$$
\begin{array}{r}
874 \\
\times \quad 2 \\
\hline
1748
\end{array}
$$

(2)
$$
\begin{array}{r}
653 \\
\times \quad 3 \\
\hline
1959
\end{array}
$$

(4)
$$
\begin{array}{r}
261 \\
\times \quad 5 \\
\hline
1305
\end{array}
$$

(6)
$$
\begin{array}{r}
692 \\
\times \quad 4 \\
\hline
2768
\end{array}
$$

## 2 Rewrite the problem vertically. Then multiply.

(1) 482 × 3

$$
\begin{array}{r}
482 \\
\times \quad 3 \\
\hline
1446
\end{array}
$$

(2) 641 × 5

$$
\begin{array}{r}
641 \\
\times \quad 5 \\
\hline
3205
\end{array}
$$

Check your answers. If you missed any problems, pick one to retry.

Check & Fix

Name Rnee  Date 6/24/24

Score 8/8

## 1 Multiply.

(1) 
$$
\begin{array}{r}
387 \\
\times \quad 4 \\
\hline
1548 \\
\end{array}
$$

(3) 
$$
\begin{array}{r}
745 \\
\times \quad 6 \\
\hline
4470 \\
\end{array}
$$

(5) 
$$
\begin{array}{r}
468 \\
\times \quad 5 \\
\hline
2340 \\
\end{array}
$$

(2) 
$$
\begin{array}{r}
652 \\
\times \quad 7 \\
\hline
4564 \\
\end{array}
$$

(4) 
$$
\begin{array}{r}
863 \\
\times \quad 9 \\
\hline
7767 \\
\end{array}
$$

(6) 
$$
\begin{array}{r}
596 \\
\times \quad 8 \\
\hline
4768 \\
\end{array}
$$

## 2 Rewrite the problem vertically. Then multiply.

(1) 478 × 3

$$
\begin{array}{r}
478 \\
\times \quad 3 \\
\hline
1434 \\
\end{array}
$$

(2) 595 × 4

$$
\begin{array}{r}
595 \\
\times \quad 4 \\
\hline
2380 \\
\end{array}
$$

Check your answers. If you missed any problems, pick one to retry.

Check & Fix

## Column Multiplication ②
3 Digit × 1 Digit ⑫

Name _Ronie_  Date 6/25/24

Score 6 / 6

**1** Multiply.

(1) ✓
```
    2 9 1
  ×     4
  ---------
  1 1 6 4
```

(2) ✓
```
    1 6 2
  ×     8
  ---------
  1 2 9 6
```

(3) ✓
```
    3 5 2
  ×     3
  ---------
  1 0 5 6
```

**2** Rewrite the problem vertically. Then multiply.

(1) ✓ 396 × 3
```
    3 9 6
  ×     3
  ---------
  1 7 8 8
```

(2) ✓ 285 × 4
```
    2 8 5
  ×     4
  ---------
  1 1 9 0    +1140
```

**3** ✓ Jonah organized his baseball card collection into 3 binders. If each binder holds 364 cards and there are no empty pages, how many cards does he have?

Jonah altogether has 1092 cards split between his 3 binders.

```
    3 6 4
  ×     3
  ---------
  1 0 9 2
```

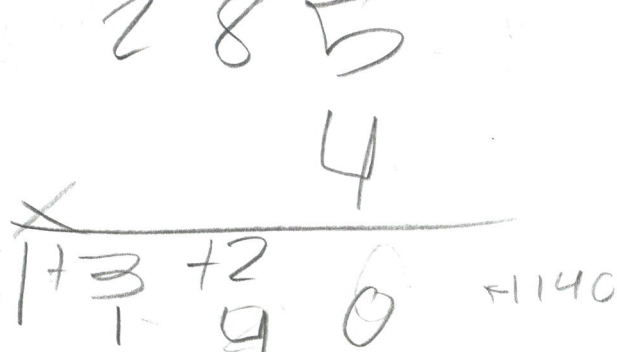

Check your answers. If you missed any problems, pick one to retry.

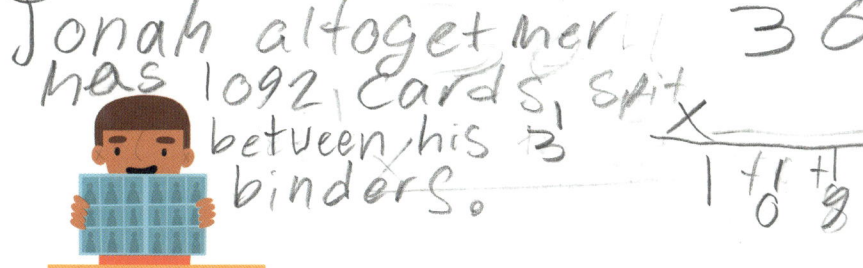

Ans. _1092_ cards

29

# 29 Column Multiplication ②

3 Digit × 1 Digit ⑬

Name: Rokee

Date: 6/25/24

Score: 8/8

## 1 Multiply.

(1) $537 \times 3 = 1611$

(2) $419 \times 6 = 2514$

(3) $726 \times 4 = 2904$

(4) $318 \times 7 = 2226$

(5) $825 \times 4 = 3300$

(6) $514 \times 8 = 4112$

## 2 Rewrite the problem vertically. Then multiply.

(1) 629 × 4

$629 \times 4 = 2516$

(2) 835 × 3

$835 \times 3 = 2505$

**Check your answers. If you missed any problems, pick one to retry.**

Check & Fix

 **Column Multiplication ②**
3 Digit × 1 Digit ⑭

**1** Multiply.

(1)
```
      792
  ×     4
  ⁺³ ⁺³
    3168
```

(3)
```
      381
  ×     6
     ⁺⁴
    2286
```

(5)
```
      581
  ×     7
   ⁺⁵
   4067
```

(2)
```
      673
  ×     3
    ⁺²
   2019
```

(4)
```
      251
  ×     8
     ⁺⁴
   2008
```

(6)
```
      762
  ×     4
    ⁺²
   3048
```

**2** Rewrite the problem vertically. Then multiply.

(1) 692 × 3

```
   693
     3
  ×
   ⁺²
  2079
```

(2) 461 × 9

```
   461
      9
  ×
  4⁺⁵149
```

Check your
answers.
If you missed
any problems,
pick one to retry.

Check & Fix

31

Name Rmée

Date 6/26/24

Score /8

**1** Multiply.

(1)
```
    3 8 9
  ×     6
  +2+5+5
  2 3 3 4
```

(3)
```
    7 7 5
  ×     4
    +2+2
  3 0 8 0
```

(5)
```
    4 8 6
  ×     7
      +4
  6 0 0 2
```

(2)
```
    5 6 8
  ×     9
  5 1 1 2
```

(4)
```
    4 5 8
  ×     9
    +4+7
  4 0 5 2
```

(6)
```
    8 3 4
  ×     6
      ×2
  5 0 0 4
```

**2** Rewrite the problem vertically. Then multiply.

(1) 263 × 8

```
    2 6 3
  ×     8
  +4+2
  2 1 0 4
```

(2) 779 × 4

```
    7 7 9
  ×     4
   +2 +3
  3 1 1 6
```

Check your answers. If you missed any problems, pick one to retry.

Check & Fix

Name _Rhoees_     Date _6/27/24_

Score _/6_

**1** Multiply.

(1)
```
    340
  ×   4
  1360
```

(2)
```
    503
  ×   7
  35⁺²21
```

(3)
```
    650
  ×   8
  5⁺⁴200
```

**2** Rewrite the problem vertically. Then multiply.

(1) 570 × 6

```
   570
 ×   6
 3⁺⁴420
```

(2) 406 × 5

```
   406
 ×   5
 20⁺³30
```

**3** A theater can seat 850 people. If a musician plays for 4 nights, what is the maximum number of people who will be able to see the show?

```
   850
 ×   4
 3⁺²400
```

Ans. 3400 people

Check your answers. If you missed any problems, pick one to retry.

Check & Fix

Name Runil

Date 6/27/24

Score /6

## 1 Multiply.

(1)
```
    1 2 4
  ×     3
  ───────
    3 8 8
```

(2) ✓
```
    8 2 3
  ×     3
  ───────
    2 4 6 9
```

(3) ✓
```
    1 4 4
  ×     9
  ───────
  1 2 9 6
```

## 2 Rewrite the problem vertically. Then multiply.

(1) 293 × 3

```
    2 9 3
  ×     3
  ───────
    8 7 9
```
✓

(2) 732 × 4

```
    7 3 2
  ×     4
  ───────
  2 9 6 8
```

## 3 Meredith has 2 pieces of rope that are 486 inches long. How many inches would the ropes be if she connected them end to end?

```
    4 8 6
  ×     2
  ───────
    9 7 2
```

486 × 2 = 972

486 + 486 = 972

400 + 400 + 80 + 80 + 12 = 972

Ans. 972 inches

Check your answers.
If you missed any problems, pick one to retry.

Check & Fix

34

## 34 Column Multiplication ②
### 3 Digit × 1 Digit ⑱

Name _Rmee_  Date _6_/_28_/_24_

Score

_/6_

**1** Multiply.

(1)  ✓
$$\begin{array}{r} 296 \\ \times\ 3 \\ \hline 888 \end{array}$$

(2) ✓
$$\begin{array}{r} 408 \\ \times\ 2 \\ \hline 816 \end{array}$$

(3)  ✓
$$\begin{array}{r} 625 \\ \times\ 3 \\ \hline 1875 \end{array}$$

**2** Rewrite the problem vertically. Then multiply.

(1) 122 × 4  ✓
$$\begin{array}{r} 122 \\ 4 \\ \times \\ \hline 488 \end{array}$$

(2) 858 × 7
$$\begin{array}{r} 858 \\ \times\ 7 \\ \hline 5956 \end{array}$$

**3** A loaf of bread weighs 625 grams. How much would 3 loaves weigh?

625 × 3 = (1875)

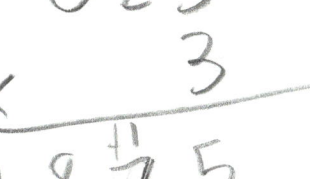
$$\begin{array}{r} 625 \\ \times\ 3 \\ \hline 1875 \end{array}$$

gms  gms  gms
625  625  625
5 lbs  5 lbs  5 lbs
5, 10, 15   15 pounds

Ans. _1875_ grams  ✓

Check your answers. If you missed any problems, pick one to retry.

Check & Fix

35

Name Renée

Date 6 /28/ 24

Score 8 / 8

## 1 Multiply. ✓

(1)
```
      2 1
  ×   4 2
```
4 2 ① 21 × 2
+ 8 4 ② 21 × 4
8 8 2 ③ Add.

(3) ✓
```
      2 4
  ×   1 2
```
4 8
2 4
2 8 8

(5) ✓
```
      1 1
  ×   5 4
```
4 4
+ 5 5
5 9 4

(2) ✓
```
      3 2
  ×   3 1
```
3 2
9 6
9 9 2

(4) ✓
```
      1 3
  ×   2 3
```
3 9
2 6
2 9 9

(6) ✓
```
      3 2
  ×   2 1
```
3 2
+ 6 4
6 7 2

## 2 Rewrite the problem vertically. Then multiply.

(1) 14 × 21 ✓

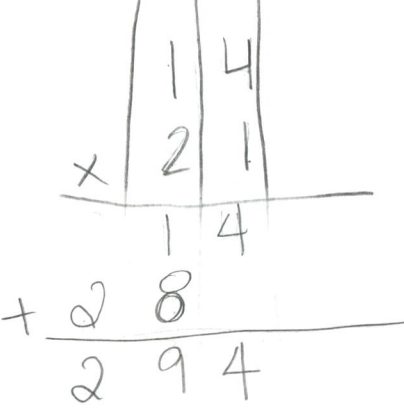

```
      1 4
  ×   2 1
      1 4
+   2 8
    2 9 4
```

(2) 33 × 12 ✓

```
      3 3
  ×   1 2
      6 6
    3 3
    3 9 6
```

Check your answers. If you missed any problems, pick one to retry.

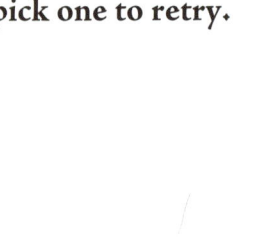

36

Name _Renee_  Date _6/29/24_

Score _8_ / _8_

## 1 Multiply.

(1)
```
      2 4
  ×   4 1
 ─────────
  [2 4]      ① 24 × 1
 [9 6]       ② 24 × 4
 [9 8 4]     ③ Add.
```

(3)
```
      1 5
  ×   2 4
 ─────────
    ⁺²6 0
  +⁺¹3 0
 ─────────
   3 6 0
```

(5)
```
      2 4
  ×   3 3
 ─────────
    ⁺¹7 2
  +⁺¹7 2
 ─────────
   7 9 2
```

(2)
```
      1 4
  ×   6 3
 ─────────
    ⁴4 2
  +⁺⁺8 4
 ─────────
   8 8 2
```

(4)
```
      1 9
  ×   4 2
 ─────────
   ⁺¹3 8      19 × 2
  ⁺³7 6        19 × 4
 +
 ─────────
  1 9 8
```

(6)
```
      4 2
  ×   2 1
 ─────────
     4 2
  +⁸8 4 2
 ─────────
   8 8 2
```

## 2 Rewrite the problem vertically. Then multiply.

(1) 27 × 32

```
    2 7
  × 3 2
 ─────────
  ⁺¹5 4
 +²8 1
 ─────────
  8 6 4
```

(2) 15 × 62

```
    1 5
  × 6 2
 ─────────
 +³3⁺¹0
 +9 0
 ─────────
  9 3 0
```

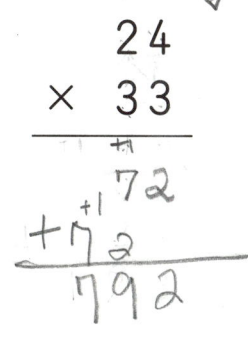

Check your answers. If you missed any problems, pick one to retry.

Check & Fix

37

Name *renée*  Date 6/29/24

Score  /6

## 1 Multiply.

(1)
```
      2 3
  ×   3 2
  ─────────
      4 6
    6 9
  ─────────
    7 3 6
```

> Don't forget to carry over when adding.

(3)
```
      3 8
  ×   2 2
  ─────────
  +1  7 6
    7 6
  ─────────
    8 3 6
```

(5)
```
      1 1
  ×   8 5
  ─────────
  +1  5 5
    8 8
  ─────────
    9 3 5
```

(2)
```
      4 2
  ×   1 2
```

(4)
```
      1 5
  ×   3 4
  ─────────
  +1  6 0
    4 5
  ─────────
    5 1 0
```

(6)
```
      1 4
  ×   3 6
  ─────────
  +1  8 4
  +1  4 2
  ─────────
    5 0 4
```

## 2 Rewrite the problem vertically. Then multiply.

(1) 21 × 43
```
    2 1
  × 4 3
  ───────
    6 3
  8 4
  ───────
  9 0 3
```

(2) 37 × 12
```
    3 7
  × 1 2
  ───────
  +1 7 4
  3 7
  ───────
  4 4 4
```

> **Check your answers.** If you missed any problems, pick one to retry.
>
> Check & Fix

38

# 38 Column Multiplication ③
## 2 Digit × 2 Digit ④

## 1 Multiply.

(1)
```
      3 2
 ×    2 8
 ─────────
    2 5 6
      6 4
 ─────────
    8 9 6
```

(2)
```
      2 4
 ×    2 6
 ─────────
      4 4
 +  5 8
 ─────────
    6 2 4
```

(3)
```
      3 5
 ×    1 4
 ─────────
      4 0
 +  4 5
 ─────────
    4 9 0
```

## 2 Rewrite the problem vertically. Then multiply.

(1) 24 × 27
```
      2 4
 ×    2 7
 ─────────
    1 6 8
 +  5 8
 ─────────
    6 4 8
```

(2) 36 × 14
```
      3 6
 ×    1 4
 ─────────
    1 4 4
 +  3 6
 ─────────
    5 0 4
```

## 3 A box of ice pops has 25 ice pops. How many ice pops are in 24 boxes?

```
      2 5
 ×    2 4
 ─────────
    1 0 0
 +  5 0 0
 ─────────
    6 0 0
```

Ans. 600 ice pops

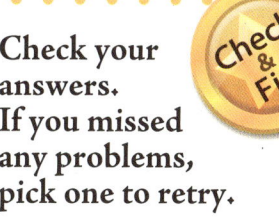

Check your answers. If you missed any problems, pick one to retry.

39

Name _Lunis_    Date 6/30/24

Score 8 / 8

## 1 Multiply.

(1)
```
    4 7 ✓
  ×  2 5
  ─────
    2 3 5
      9 4
  + ─────
  1 1 7 5
```

(2) ✓
```
    2 8
  ×  3 7
  ─────
    1 9 6
      8 4
  + ─────
  1, 0 3 6
```

(3) ✓
```
    2 3
  ×  4 8
  ─────
    1 8 4
      9 2
  + ─────
  1 1 0 4
```

(4) ✓
```
    8 4
  ×  1 3
  ─────
    2 5 2
  + 8 4 0
  ─────
  1 0 9 2
```

(5) ✓
```
    2 6
  ×  3 9
  ─────
    2 3 4
  + 7 8 0
  ─────
  1 0 1 4
```

(6) ✓
```
    4 5
  ×  2 6
  ─────
    2 7 0
  + 9 0 0
  ─────
  1 1 7 0
```

## 2 Rewrite the problem vertically. Then multiply.

(1) 32 × 36
```
    3 2 ✓
  ×  3 6
  ─────
    1 9 2
  + 9 6 0
  ─────
  1 1 5 2
```

(2) 39 × 27
```
    3 9 ✓
  ×  2 7
  ─────
    2 7 3
  + 7 8 0
  ─────
  1 0 5 3
```

Check your answers. If you missed any problems, pick one to retry.

Check & Fix

40

## 1 Multiply.

(1)
```
     3 6
  ×  4 1
  ───────
    3 6
  1 4 4
+
  1 4 7 6
```

(3)
```
     2 3
  ×  8 2
  ───────
      4 6
+ 1 8 4
  ───────
  1 8 8 6
```

(5)
```
     4 6
  ×  7 1
  ───────
      4 6
+ 3 2 2
  ───────
  3 2 6 6
```

(2)
```
     2 7
  ×  5 3
  ───────
    8 1
  1 2 5
+
  1 3 3 1
```

(4)
```
     3 5
  ×  4 2
  ───────
    7 0
  1 4 0
  ───────
  1 4 7 0
```

(6)
```
     3 4
  ×  6 2
  ───────
    6 8
  2 0 4
  ───────
  2 1 0 8
```

## 2 Rewrite the problem vertically. Then multiply.

(1) 24 × 83

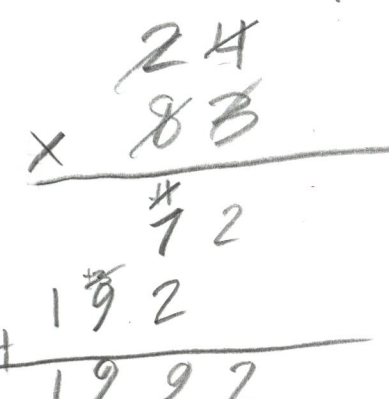

```
     2 4
  ×  8 3
  ───────
    7 2
  1 9 2
+
  1 9 9 2
```

(2) 47 × 32

```
     4 7
  ×  3 2
  ───────
    9 4
  1 4 1
+
  1 5 0 4
```

Check your answers. If you missed any problems, pick one to retry.

Check & Fix

41

Name _Renea_   Date 7 / 1 / 24

Score 8 / 8

## 1 Multiply.

(1) ✓
```
      36
   ×  54
   ¹ ²
    144
   ¹ ³
   180
   ____
  1944
```

(3) ✓
```
      45
   ×  36
   ⁴¹
    270
  + 135 0
  _____
   1620
```

(5) ✓
```
      34
   ×  59
  ⁴
    306
  + 170
  _____
   2006
```

(2) ✓
```
      42
   ×  67
  ⁴¹
    294
  + 2520
  _____
   2814
```

(4) ✓
```
      83
   ×  64
  ⁴¹ ¹
    342
   4980
  _____
   5312
```

(6) ✓
```
      48
   ×  65
  ⁴ ⁴
    240
  + 2880
  _____
   3120
```

## 2 Rewrite the problem vertically. Then multiply.

(1) 28 × 46 ✓
```
      28
   ×  46
    168
  + 1120
  _____
   1288
```

(2) 76 × 59 ✓
```
      76
   ×  59
    684
  + 3880
  _____
   4484
```

Check your answers.
If you missed any problems, pick one to retry.

Check & Fix

42

# 42 Column Multiplication ③
## 2 Digit × 2 Digit ⑧

Name _Rumie_  Date _M_ / _2_ / _24_

Score _6_ / _6_

**1** Multiply.

(1)
```
      60
   ×  28
   ┌───────┐
   │ 4 8 0 │
   ├───────┤
   │ 1 2 0 │
   ├───────┤
   │ 1 6 8 0│
   └───────┘
```

(2)
```
      50
   ×  17
      350
   +    5
   ──────
      850
```

(3)
```
      40
   ×  35
      1 2 0 8
   ────────
      1400
```

**2** Rewrite the problem vertically. Then multiply.

(1) 40 × 87
```
     40
     87
   ×
    280
   3200
  +
  3480
```

(2) 80 × 65
```
     80
   × 65
   + 400
     480
   ──────
   5200
```

**3** A packet of flower seeds contains 60 seeds. How many seeds are in 34 packets?

```
     60
     34
   ×
  + 240
   180
  ×
   2040
```

Ans. _2040_ seeds

43

Name *Lenier*  Date 7 /2 /24

Score 6 / 6

## 1 Multiply.

(1)

```
    2 1
  × 3 0
  ─────
  6 3 0
```

> ① Instead of calculating ×0, you can simply put a 0 in the ones place.

② 21 × 3

(2)

```
    4 9
  × 2 0
  ─────
+ 9 8 0
  ─────
  9 8 0
```

(3)

```
    7 3
  × 6 0
  ─────
  4 3 8 0
  ─────
  4 3 8 0
```

## 2 Rewrite the problem vertically. Then multiply.

(1) 67 × 80

```
    6 7
    8 0
  × ─────
+ 5 3 6
  ─────
  5 3 6
```

(2) 45 × 60

```
    4 5
  × 6 0
  ─────
+ 2 7 0
  ─────
  2 7 0
```

## 3 Each classroom in an elementary school has 24 desks. How many desks are in 30 classrooms?

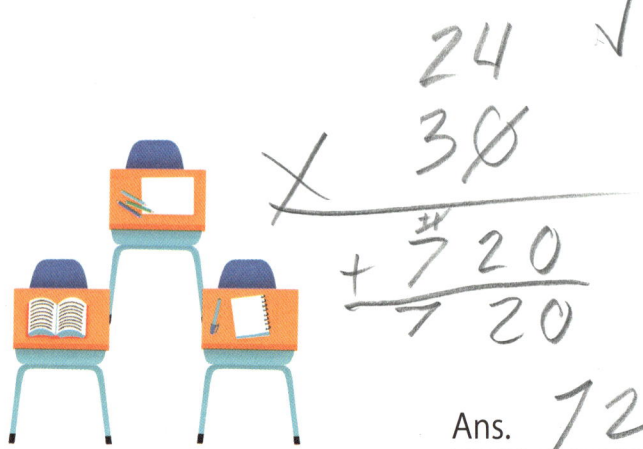

```
    2 4
    3 0
  × ─────
+ 7 2 0
  ─────
  7 2 0
```

Ans. 720 desks

> Check your answers. If you missed any problems, pick one to retry.
>
> Check & Fix

44

## Column Multiplication ③
### 2 Digit × 2 Digit ⑩

Name _kdfld_

Date 7 / 3 / 24

Score 6 / 6

**1** Multiply. ✓

(1)
```
    1 8
  × 3 2
  ─────
  5 3 6
    4 0
  ─────
  5 7 6
```

(2)
```
    2 4
  × 6 3
  ─────
  1 4 7 2
    4 0
  ─────
  1 5 1 2
```

(3)
```
    2 7
  × 3 8
  ─────
  2 1 6
  8 1 0
  ─────
  1 0 2 6
```

**2** Rewrite the problem vertically. Then multiply.

(1) 25 × 32 ✓
```
    2 5
  × 3 2
  ─────
  5 0
  7 5 0
  ─────
  8 0 0
```

(2) 70 × 64 ✓
```
      7 0
  ×   6 4
  ───────
  4 4 8 0
      0 0
  ───────
  4 4 8 0
```

**3** A box of straws contains 32 straws. How many straws are in 21 boxes? ✓

```
    3 2
    2 1
  × ───
  6 3 2
    4 0
  ─────
  6 7 2
```

Ans. 672 straws

Check your answers.
If you missed any problems, pick one to retry.

Check & Fix

45

# Column Multiplication ③
## 2 Digit × 2 Digit ⑪

Name _kinee_

Date 7 /3 /24

Score 6 /6

**1** Multiply.

(1)
```
    1 2
  ×  2 4
    4 8
× 2 4 0
  2 8 8
```

(2)
```
    4 3
  ×  2 3
    1 2 9
+   8 6 0
    9 8 9
```

(3)
```
      3 0
  ×   9 6
    1 8 0
+ 2 7 0 0
  2 8 8 0
```

**2** Rewrite the problem vertically. Then multiply.

(1) 36 × 28
```
      3 6
  ×   2 8
    2 8 8
+   7 2 0
  1 0 0 8
```

(2) 85 × 23
```
      8 5
  ×   2 3
    2 5 5
+ 1 7 0 0
  1 9 5 5
```

**3** A box contains 23 toy cars. How many toy cars would be in 28 boxes?

```
      2 3
  ×   2 8
    1 8 4
+   4 6 0
    6 4 4
```

Ans. _____ toy cars

Check your answers. If you missed any problems, pick one to retry.

Check & Fix

46

2 Digit × 2 Digit ⑫

Name _Renie_  Date 7 / 4 /24

Score ___ / 6

**1** Multiply.

(1)
```
    24
  × 34
   96
  120
  816
```

(2)
```
    32
  × 69
   288
  1920
  2208
```

(3)
```
    35
  × 40
  1400
   00
  1400
```

**2** Rewrite the problem vertically. Then multiply.

(1) 34 × 25
```
   34
 × 25
  170
  680
  850
```

(2) 16 × 24
```
   16
 × 24
   64
  32
  384
```

**3** Farrah bought 70 packets of seeds. If each packet has 45 seeds, how many seeds does she have in total?

```
   70
 × 45
  350
```

Ans. _____ seeds

Ans. 3150 seeds

Check your answers. If you missed any problems, pick one to retry.

Check & Fix

47

# 47 Final Practice
## Mental Arithmetic

Name *Renee* ♡

Date  7 /4 /24

Score  / 11

**1** Multiply.

(1) $9 \times 2 = 18$ ✓

(2) $6 \times 5 = 30$ ✓

(3) $7 \times 6 = 42$ ✓

(4) $1 \times 8 = 8$ ✓

(5) $3 \times 10 = 30$ ✓

(6) $4 \times 11 = 44$ ✓

(7) $12 \times 1 = 12$ ✓

(8) $8 \times 0 = 0$

(9) $100 \times 7 = 700$ ✓

(10) $80 \times 3 = 240$ ✓

**2** James bought 7 pairs of socks for $4 each. How much did he spend?

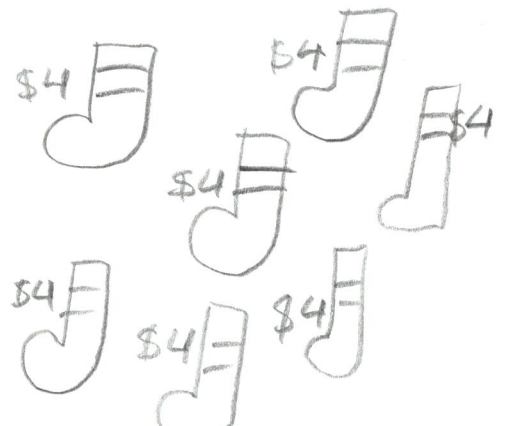

$4 \times 7 = 28$ ✓

Ans. $ 28

Check
& Fix

**Check your answers. If you missed any problems, pick one to retry.**

Name _Kruss_

Date ___/___/___

Score ___/6

**1** Multiply.

(1)
```
    28  ✓
×    3
   ⁺²8 4
+
   8 4
```

(2)
```
    50
×    4
  250
+
  250
```

(3)
```
    58  ✓
×    7
  ⁺⁵40 6
×
  4 0 6
```

**2** Rewrite the problem vertically. Then multiply.

(1) 11 × 9   ✓
```
   1 1
      9
×
+  9 9
   9 9
```

(2) 47 × 4   ✓
```
   4 7
      4
×
  ⁺² 
+ 1 8 8
  1 8 8
```

**3** A gardener is planting sunflowers. If she plants 4 rows with 26 sunflowers in each row, how many sunflowers will she have?

```
    2 6
      4
×
  ⁺²
  1 0 4
  1 0 4
```
Ans. __104__ sunflowers

Check your answers. If you missed any problems, pick one to retry.

Check & Fix

Name _three_

Date ___/___/___

Score ___/6

**1** Multiply.

(1)
```
   1 0 3 ✓
 ×     3
 ─────────
   3 0 9
```

(2)
```
   2 1 9 ✓
 ×     4
 ─────────
   8 7⁺³ 6
```

(3)
```
   1 8 1 ✓
 ×     6
 ─────────
 1⁺⁴ 0 8 6
```

**2** Rewrite the problem vertically. Then multiply.

(1) 1 1 3 × 8

```
   1 1 3 ✓
 ×     8
 ─────────
  ⁺¹ ⁺¹² 
   9 0 4
```

(2) 4 1 0 × 3

```
   4 1 0 ✓
 ×     3
 ─────────
 1 2 3 0
```

**3** An elementary school bought 514 boxes of crayons. If there are 8 crayons in each box, how many crayons are there in total?

```
   5 1 4 ✓
 ×     8
 ─────────
  ⁺¹ ⁺³ 
 4 1 1 2
```

Ans. _4112_ crayons

**Check your answers.** If you missed any problems, pick one to retry.

Check & Fix

50

Name Rưới ♡

Date / /

Score

/ 6

 Multiply.

(1)
```
      2 4  ✓
    ×  6 4
    #  9 6
    1 4 4 0
  +
    1 5 3 6
```

(2)
```
      8 0  ✓
    ×  3 2
      1 6 0
  + 2 4 0 0
    2 5 6 0
```

(3)
```
      2 2  ✓
    ×  2 4
  +   8 8
      4 4 0
      5 2 8
```

**2** Rewrite the problem vertically. Then multiply.

(1) 32 × 12

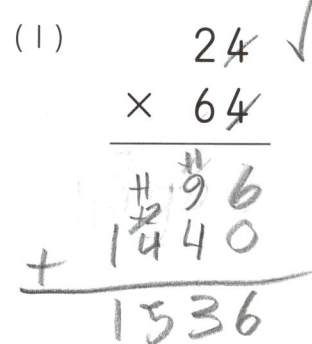
```
      3 2
    ×  1 2
        6 4
   +  3 2 0    → 384
```

(2) 46 × 90

```
      4 6
    ×  9 0
        0  0
   +  3 6 4  0   → 3640
```

**3** Mrs. Jones placed 14 sheets of paper into a folder. If she needs to make 36 folders, one for each of her students, how many sheets of paper does she need?

```
        1 4
      ×  3 6
        8 4
      4 2 0
      5 0 4
```

Ans. 504 sheets

Check your answers. If you missed any problems, pick one to retry.

Check & Fix

51

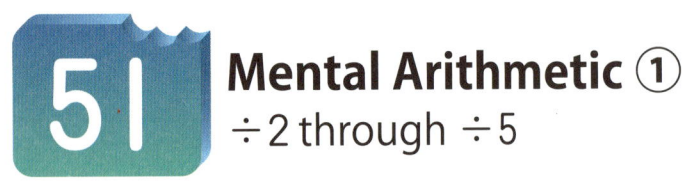

## 51 Mental Arithmetic ①
÷ 2 through ÷ 5

Name

Date / /

Score / 11

**1** Divide.

(1)  8 ÷ 2 =

(2)  12 ÷ 2 =

(3)  16 ÷ 2 =

(4)  6 ÷ 3 =

(5)  21 ÷ 3 =

(6)  4 ÷ 4 =

(7)  20 ÷ 4 =

(8)  36 ÷ 4 =

(9)  15 ÷ 5 =

(10)  40 ÷ 5 =

**2** Warren has 12 bananas. If he divides them evenly among his 3 friends, how many will each friend get?

Ans.                    bananas

**Check your answers. If you missed any problems, pick one to retry.**

52

## 52 Mental Arithmetic ①
÷6 through ÷10, ÷1, and 0÷

Name

Date ___/___/___

Score ___/11

**1** Divide.

(1) $18 \div 6 =$

(2) $48 \div 6 =$

(3) $28 \div 7 =$

(4) $49 \div 7 =$

(5) $40 \div 8 =$

(6) $8 \div 8 =$

(7) $18 \div 9 =$

(8) $60 \div 10 =$

(9) $9 \div 1 =$

(10) $0 \div 1 =$

**2** Raymond has 72 gumballs. He splits them evenly among 8 of his friends. How many gumballs does each friend get?

Ans. _____ gumballs

**Check your answers. If you missed any problems, pick one to retry.**

53

**1** Divide.

(1) $5 \div 2 =$ ___ R ___      (6) $6 \div 4 =$

(2) $7 \div 2 =$ ___ R ___      (7) $19 \div 4 =$

(3) $13 \div 2 =$ ___ R ___      (8) $38 \div 4 =$

(4) $8 \div 3 =$              (9) $23 \div 5 =$

(5) $25 \div 3 =$             (10) $39 \div 5 =$

**2** A farmer has 25 carrots. If she feeds each of her 3 goats the same number of carrots, how many carrots will each goat get, and will there be any carrots leftover?

Ans. ___ carrots, ___ remain(s)

 Check your answers. If you missed any problems, pick one to retry.

54

**54** **Mental Arithmetic** ①
÷6 through ÷9 with Remainders

Name

Date
/ /

Score
/ 11

1 Divide.

(1) $14 \div 6 =$

(2) $17 \div 6 =$

(3) $46 \div 6 =$

(4) $8 \div 7 =$

(5) $59 \div 7 =$

(6) $20 \div 8 =$

(7) $33 \div 8 =$

(8) $69 \div 8 =$

(9) $31 \div 9 =$

(10) $78 \div 9 =$

2 Lola made 45 cookies for her family. If she divides the cookies equally among her 6 family members, how many cookies will each person get? How many will be leftover?

Ans. _____ cookies, _____ remain(s)

Check & Fix

**Check your answers. If you missed any problems, pick one to retry.**

55

# 55 Mental Arithmetic ① 
## Division of Tens

**1** Divide.

(1)  $20 \div 2 =$

(2)  $30 \div 3 =$

(3)  $70 \div 7 =$

(4)  $40 \div 2 =$

(5)  $60 \div 3 =$

(6)  $90 \div 3 =$

(7)  $80 \div 2 =$

(8)  $60 \div 2 =$

(9)  $50 \div 5 =$

(10)  $80 \div 4 =$

**2** Henry is dividing 60 books between 3 shelves. If he puts the same number of books on each shelf, how many books will be on each shelf?

Ans.                books

 **Check & Fix** Check your answers. If you missed any problems, pick one to retry.

Name

Date      /      /

Score

/ | |

1 Divide.

(1)  $6 \div 3 =$

(2)  $14 \div 2 =$

(3)  $35 \div 7 =$

(4)  $9 \div 1 =$

(5)  $5 \div 2 =$

(6)  $23 \div 5 =$

(7)  $11 \div 4 =$

(8)  $70 \div 8 =$

(9)  $34 \div 9 =$

(10)  $80 \div 2 =$

2 Mary is arranging 14 books evenly on 2 shelves. How many books will be on each shelf?

Ans.              books

 **Check your answers. If you missed any problems, pick one to retry.**

**1** Divide.

(1) $40 \div 5 =$

(2) $16 \div 4 =$

(3) $70 \div 10 =$

(4) $48 \div 8 =$

(5) $10 \div 3 =$

(6) $31 \div 4 =$

(7) $13 \div 2 =$

(8) $37 \div 7 =$

(9) $8 \div 6 =$

(10) $30 \div 3 =$

**2** Kylie made 36 cupcakes. She placed them evenly in 4 boxes. How many cupcakes did she put in each box?

Ans.                    cupcakes

**Check your answers. If you missed any problems, pick one to retry.**

58
**Mental Arithmetic** ①
Mixed ③

Name

Date
/ /

Score
/ 11

1 Divide.

(1) $12 \div 3 =$

(6) $23 \div 3 =$

(2) $20 \div 5 =$

(7) $17 \div 8 =$

(3) $72 \div 9 =$

(8) $59 \div 6 =$

(4) $0 \div 2 =$

(9) $26 \div 7 =$

(5) $31 \div 5 =$

(10) $40 \div 2 =$

2 Frankie read 72 pages in his book today. That is 9 times more than he read yesterday. How many pages did Frankie read yesterday?

Ans. _____ pages

 Check your answers.
If you missed any
problems, pick one
to retry.

## 59 Column Division ①
### 2 Digit ÷ 1 Digit ①

Name

Date      /      /

Score

          / 6

**1** Divide.

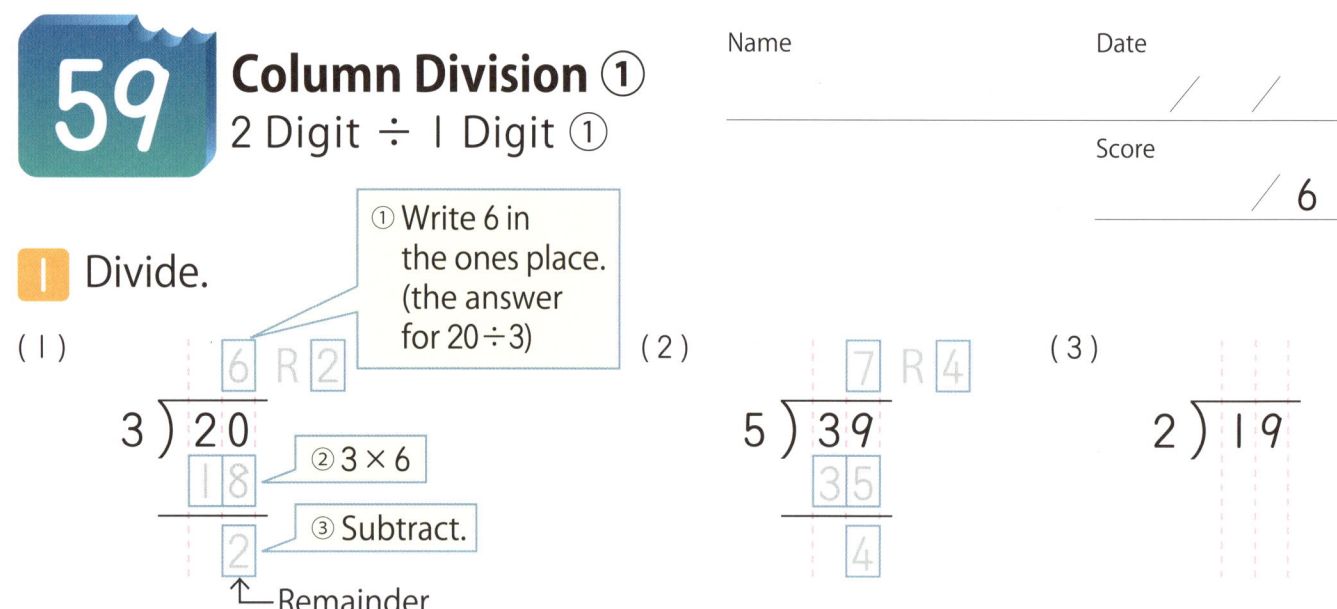

( 1 )

① Write 6 in the ones place. (the answer for 20 ÷ 3)

```
      6 R 2
  3 ) 2 0
      1 8      ② 3 × 6
      ─────
        2      ③ Subtract.
        ↑
        Remainder
```

( 2 )

```
      7 R 4
  5 ) 3 9
      3 5
      ───
        4
```

( 3 )

```
  2 ) 1 9
```

**2** Rewrite the problem vertically. Then divide.

( 1 ) 40 ÷ 8

```
  8 ) 4 0
```

( 2 ) 50 ÷ 6

**3** Mr. Morgan has 42 loose tea bags that he is dividing into boxes. He places 6 bags into each box. How many boxes of tea can he make?

42 ÷ 6 =

Check your answers. If you missed any problems, pick one to retry.

Check & Fix

Ans. _____ boxes

60

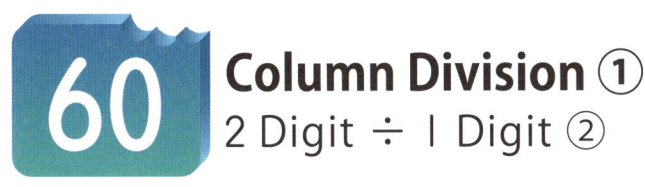

## 60 Column Division ①
## 2 Digit ÷ 1 Digit ②

Name

Date    /    /

Score    / 6

**1** Divide.

( 1 )

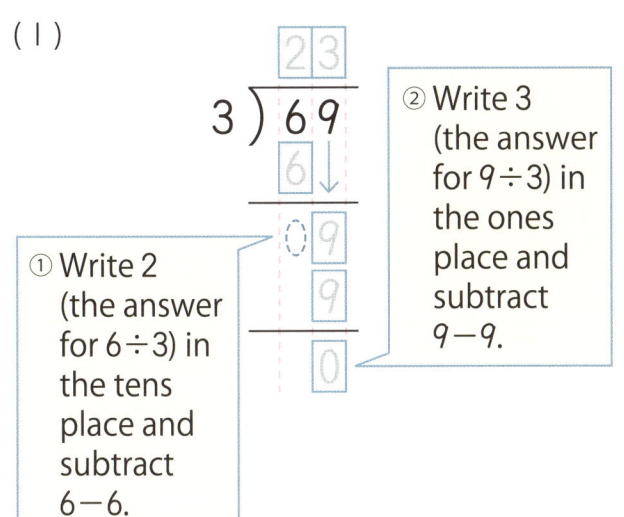

① Write 2 (the answer for 6÷3) in the tens place and subtract 6−6.

② Write 3 (the answer for 9÷3) in the ones place and subtract 9−9.

( 2 )

2 ) 4 6

( 3 )

4 ) 8 4

**2** Rewrite the problem vertically. Then divide.

( 1 ) 8 2 ÷ 2

) 8 2

( 2 ) 7 7 ÷ 7

**3** There are 63 kids in a soccer league. If they are divided into 3 teams, how many kids will each team have?

Ans. _____ kids

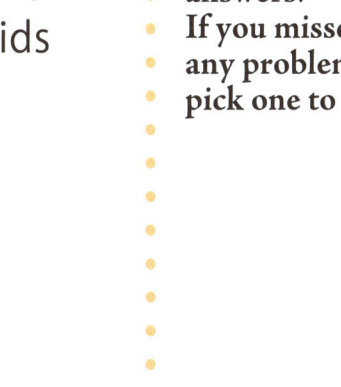

Check your answers.
If you missed any problems, pick one to retry.

**1** Divide.

(1)

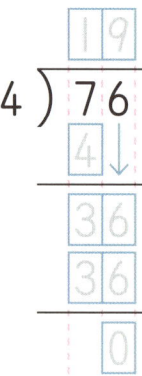

```
     1 9
  4)7 6
    4
    3 6
    3 6
      0
```

(2)

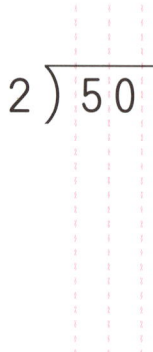

```
  2)5 0
```

(3)

```
  7)9 1
```

**2** Rewrite the problem vertically. Then divide.

(1) 76 ÷ 2

(2) 92 ÷ 4

**3** Alex has 75 lollipops at his party. He divides them equally among his 5 friends. How many lollipops does each friend get?

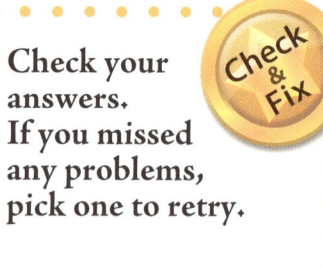

Check your answers. If you missed any problems, pick one to retry.

Check & Fix

Ans. _____ lollipops

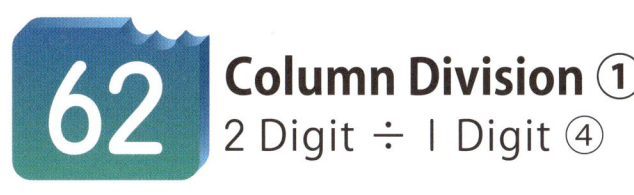

## Column Division ①
## 2 Digit ÷ 1 Digit ④

**1** Divide.

(1)

```
        2 2  R 1
    4 ) 8 9
        8 ↓
        0 9
          8
          1
```

(2)

```
    2 ) 6 5
```

(3)

```
    3 ) 9 8
```

**2** Rewrite the problem vertically. Then divide.

(1) $69 \div 6$

(2) $49 \div 2$

**3** Lindsay separated 64 potatoes evenly into 3 bags. How many potatoes are in each bag and how many are leftover?

Check your answers. If you missed any problems, pick one to retry.

Check & Fix

Ans. _____ potatoes, _____ remain(s)

Name

Date / /

Score / 6

**1** Divide.

(1)
```
      1 5  R 1
   3) 4 6
      3↓
      1 6
      1 5
        1
```

(2)
```
   6) 9 8
```

(3)
```
   2) 7 1
```

**2** Rewrite the problem vertically. Then divide.

(1) 70 ÷ 4

(2) 85 ÷ 3

**3** David needs to cut 84 cm of tape into 5 cm pieces for his project. How many pieces can he make and how much tape will be leftover?

Ans. _____ pieces, _____ cm remain(s)

Name

Date / /

Score / 6

**1** Divide.

(1)

```
      2 0 R 3
  4 ) 8 3
      8 ↓
      0 3
```

(2)

```
  7 ) 7 5
```

(3)

```
  2 ) 8 1
```

**2** Rewrite the problem vertically. Then divide.

(1) 60 ÷ 2

(2) 42 ÷ 4

**3** Paul wants to cut an 82-inch-long ribbon into 4-inch-long pieces. How many pieces will he have and how many inches will be leftover?

Check your answers. If you missed any problems, pick one to retry.

Check & Fix

Ans.          pieces,          inch(es) remain(s)

Name

Date        /        /

Score        / 6

**1** Divide.

( 1 )

4 ⟌ 2 3

( 2 )

6 ⟌ 8 4

( 3 )

2 ⟌ 6 1

**2** Rewrite the problem vertically. Then divide.

( 1 )  68 ÷ 2

( 2 )  90 ÷ 7

—

**3** At a school Sports Day, 56 children were divided into teams of 7. How many teams will there be?

Check your answers. If you missed any problems, pick one to retry.

Check & Fix

Ans. _____ teams

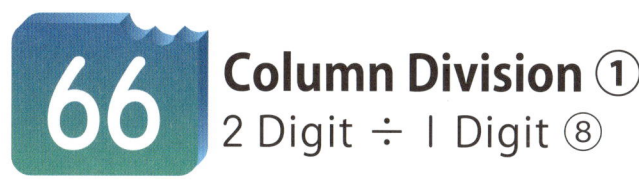

# 66 Column Division ①
## 2 Digit ÷ 1 Digit ⑧

**1** Divide.

( 1 )

$$9\overline{)34}$$

( 2 )

$$3\overline{)93}$$

( 3 )

$$5\overline{)84}$$

**2** Rewrite the problem vertically. Then divide.

( 1 )  $87 \div 3$

( 2 )  $97 \div 3$

**3** Laura made 93 bracelets, so she could give her classmates 3 each. How many classmates does she have?

Check your answers.
If you missed any problems, pick one to retry.

Check & Fix

Ans. _____ classmates

# 67 Column Division ①
## 2 Digit ÷ 1 Digit ⑨

Name

Date
/ /

Score
/ 6

**1** Divide.

( 1 )

3 ) 6 5

( 2 )

4 ) 9 9

( 3 )

5 ) 5 0

**2** Rewrite the problem vertically. Then divide.

( 1 )  1 4 ÷ 4

( 2 )  7 5 ÷ 5

**3** A supermarket has 92 shopping carts. They want to arrange the shopping carts into 3 equal rows. How many carts will be in each row and how many carts will be leftover?

Check your answers. If you missed any problems, pick one to retry.

Check & Fix

Ans.                carts,            remain(s)

# 68 Column Division ②
## 3 Digit ÷ 1 Digit ①

**1** Divide.

(1)

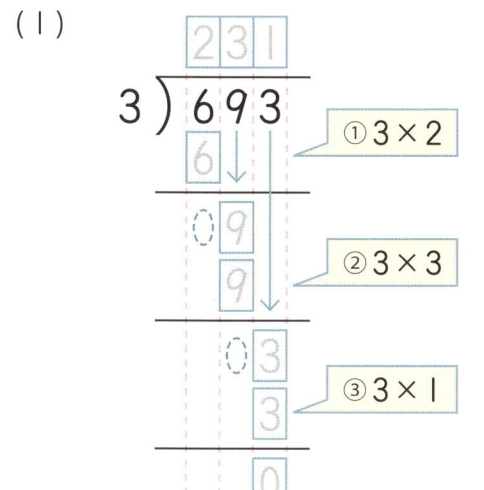

$$3\overline{)693}$$

① 3 × 2

② 3 × 3

③ 3 × 1

(2)

$$2\overline{)628}$$

(3)

$$4\overline{)884}$$

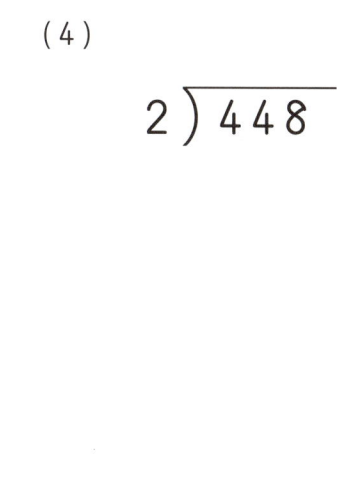

(4)

$$2\overline{)448}$$

(5)

$$3\overline{)969}$$

**2** Rewrite the problem vertically. Then divide.

(1) $262 \div 2$

(2) $996 \div 3$

Check your answers. If you missed any problems, pick one to retry.

Check & Fix

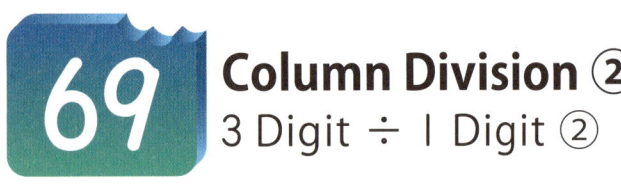

## 69 Column Division ②
### 3 Digit ÷ 1 Digit ②

Name _____

Date ___ / ___ / ___

Score ___ / 7

**1** Divide.

(1)
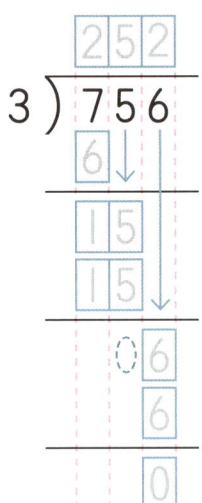

$$3 \overline{)756}$$

(2)

$$4 \overline{)872}$$

(3)

$$5 \overline{)685}$$

(4)

$$2 \overline{)592}$$

(5)

$$3 \overline{)468}$$

**2** Rewrite the problem vertically. Then divide.

(1) $942 \div 6$     (2) $672 \div 3$

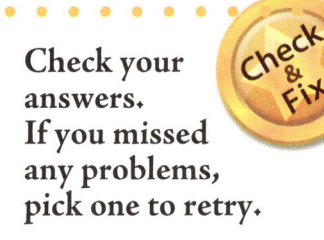

Check your answers.
If you missed any problems, pick one to retry.

# 70 Column Division ②
## 3 Digit ÷ I Digit ③

**1** Divide.

( I )

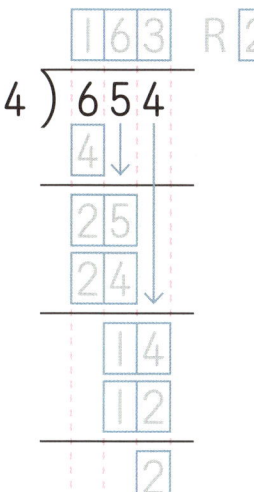

163 R 2

4 ) 6 5 4

( 2 )

2 ) 8 7 I

( 4 )

3 ) 6 8 2

( 3 )

6 ) 7 4 0

( 5 )

6 ) 7 4 0

**2** Rewrite the problem vertically. Then divide.

( I ) 9 3 8 ÷ 3          ( 2 ) 7 0 7 ÷ 4

Check your answers.
If you missed any problems, pick one to retry.

Check & Fix

Name

Date / /

Score / 6

**1** Divide.

(1)

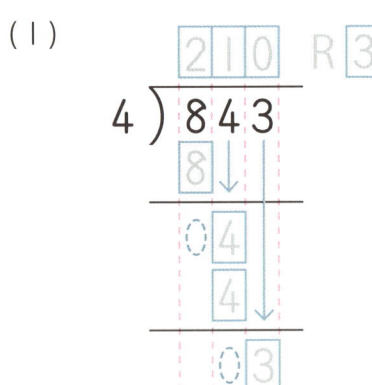

```
    2 1 0 R 3
 4 ) 8 4 3
    8 ↓
    0 4
      4 ↓
      0 3
```

(2)

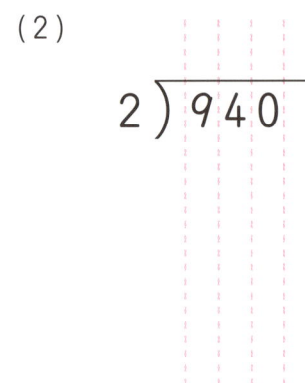

```
 2 ) 9 4 0
```

(3)

```
 6 ) 7 8 5
```

**2** Rewrite the problem vertically. Then divide.

(1) 5 4 1 ÷ 3

(2) 6 0 0 ÷ 5

**3** Ashley has 845 oz of juice. If she pours 6 oz into glasses, how many glasses can she make and how much juice will be leftover?

Ans.            glasses,        oz remain(s)

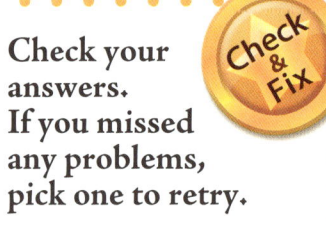

Check your answers. If you missed any problems, pick one to retry.

72

# 72 Column Division ②
## 3 Digit ÷ 1 Digit ⑤

**1** Divide.

(1)

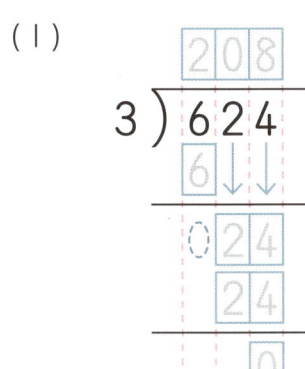

3 ) 6 2 4

(3)

7 ) 7 2 9

(5)

3 ) 9 0 2

(2)

2 ) 8 0 5

(4)

4 ) 8 3 0

(6)

2 ) 6 1 7

**2** Rewrite the problem vertically. Then divide.

(1) 8 1 2 ÷ 4

(2) 6 2 2 ÷ 6

Check your answers. If you missed any problems, pick one to retry.

Check & Fix

Name

Date
/ /

Score
/ 8

**1** Divide.

( 1 )

$$4 \overline{)\ 284}$$

( 2 )

$$7 \overline{)\ 429}$$

( 3 )

$$3 \overline{)\ 156}$$

( 4 )

$$6 \overline{)\ 547}$$

( 5 )

$$5 \overline{)\ 305}$$

( 6 )

$$2 \overline{)\ 183}$$

**2** Rewrite the problem vertically. Then divide.

( 1 ) $218 \div 3$

( 2 ) $272 \div 8$

Check your answers. If you missed any problems, pick one to retry.

Check & Fix

74

## 74 Column Division ②
### 3 Digit ÷ 1 Digit ⑦

## 1 Divide.

(1)

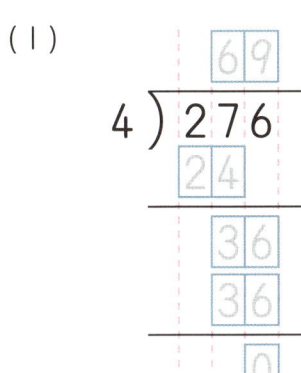

$$4\overline{)276}$$

(3)

$$6\overline{)504}$$

(5)

$$8\overline{)500}$$

(2)

$$3\overline{)169}$$

(4)

$$5\overline{)320}$$

(6)

$$9\overline{)128}$$

## 2 Rewrite the problem vertically. Then divide.

(1) $458 \div 6$

(2) $300 \div 4$

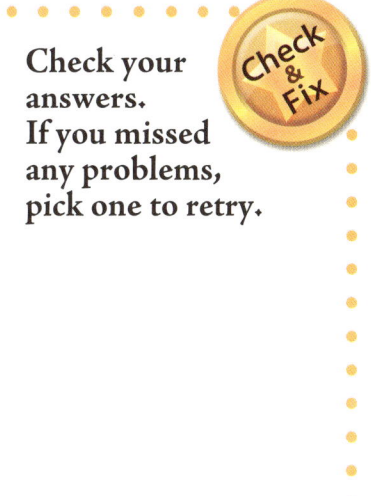

Check your answers. If you missed any problems, pick one to retry.

**1** Divide.

(1)

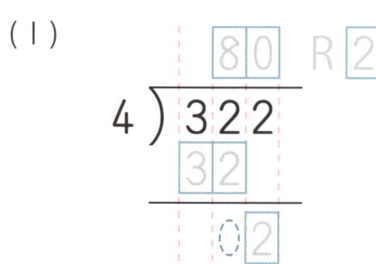

```
    80 R2
4) 322
    32
    02
```

(2)

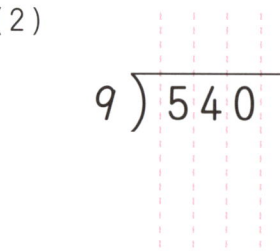

```
9) 540
```

(3)

```
3) 210
```

**2** Rewrite the problem vertically. Then divide.

(1) 564 ÷ 8

(2) 360 ÷ 4

**3** A farmer picked 180 peaches. If she divides 6 peaches equally into crates, how many crates can she make?

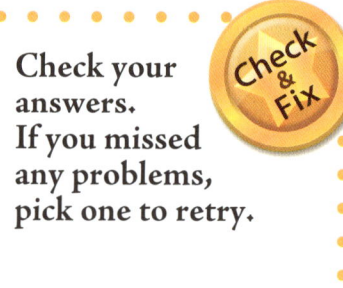

Check your answers. If you missed any problems, pick one to retry.

Ans. _____ crates

## 76 Column Division ②
### 3 Digit ÷ 1 Digit ⑨

Name

Date      /      /

Score      / 6

**1** Divide.

(1)

$$2 \overline{)\ 5\ 3\ 4}$$

(2)

$$7 \overline{)\ 9\ 1\ 4}$$

(3)

$$3 \overline{)\ 2\ 4\ 7}$$

**2** Rewrite the problem vertically. Then divide.

(1) $888 \div 4$

(2) $354 \div 7$

**3** A 462-inch piece of rope is cut in half. How long is each piece?

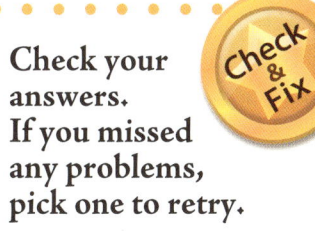

Check your answers. If you missed any problems, pick one to retry.

Ans. _____ inches

**Column Division ②**
3 Digit ÷ 1 Digit ⑩

Name

Date       /       /

Score       / 6

**1** Divide.

( 1 )

$$5 \overline{)\ 6\ 1\ 5}$$

( 2 )

$$6 \overline{)\ 7\ 4\ 3}$$

( 3 )

$$6 \overline{)\ 1\ 2\ 5}$$

**2** Rewrite the problem vertically. Then divide.

( 1 )  $462 \div 2$

( 2 )  $619 \div 6$

**3** Michelle has 743 yards of yarn. If she divides the yarn into 3 equal balls, how many yards would each ball be and how many yards of yarn would she have leftover?

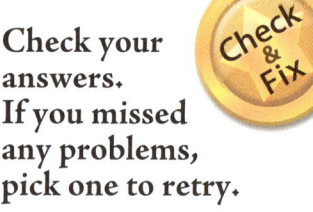

Check your answers.
If you missed any problems, pick one to retry.

Ans. _____ yards, _____ remain(s)

**1** Divide.

( 1 )

$$3 \overline{)645}$$

( 2 )

$$3 \overline{)482}$$

( 3 )

$$4 \overline{)259}$$

**2** Rewrite the problem vertically. Then divide.

( 1 ) $745 \div 3$

( 2 ) $825 \div 4$

**3** Mr. Glen has 128 colored pencils. If he divides the pencils evenly among his 9 students, how many pencils will each student get and how many will be left?

Check your answers. If you missed any problems, pick one to retry.

Check & Fix

Ans.          colored pencils,          remain(s)

## Mental Arithmetic ②
### 2 Digit ÷ 2 Digit ①

Name

Date     /     /

Score     / 11

**1** Divide.

(1)  $20 \div 10 =$

(6)  $80 \div 40 =$

(2)  $60 \div 20 =$

(7)  $50 \div 10 =$

(3)  $40 \div 20 =$

(8)  $70 \div 10 =$

(4)  $90 \div 30 =$

(9)  $60 \div 30 =$

(5)  $30 \div 10 =$

(10)  $80 \div 20 =$

**2** Aaron cut a 60-inch board into 20-inch pieces. How many pieces can he make?

Ans.                    pieces

**Check your answers. If you missed any problems, pick one to retry.**

# 80 Mental Arithmetic ②
## 2 Digit ÷ 2 Digit ②

**1** Divide.

(1) $30 \div 20 =$

(2) $90 \div 40 =$

(3) $50 \div 30 =$

(4) $70 \div 20 =$

(5) $70 \div 30 =$

(6) $60 \div 40 =$

(7) $50 \div 20 =$

(8) $80 \div 30 =$

(9) $90 \div 20 =$

(10) $70 \div 40 =$

**2** Kevin has $90. He wants to buy some model airplane sets that cost $40 each. How many sets can he buy and how much money will he have leftover?

Ans. _____ sets, $ _____ remain(s)

 Check your answers. If you missed any problems, pick one to retry.

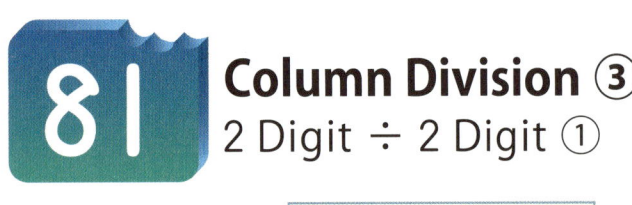

## Column Division ③
### 2 Digit ÷ 2 Digit ①

Name

Date

Score

/ 8

**1** Divide.

( 1 )

> ① Write 4 in the ones place.
> (You can estimate using 80÷20.)

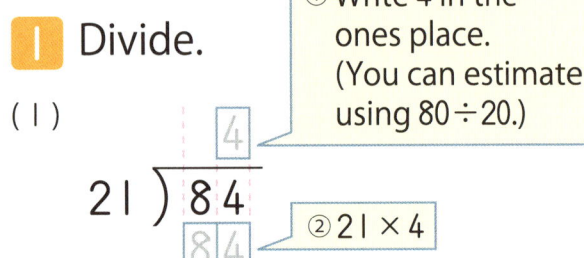

```
      4
21 ) 8 4    ② 21 × 4
   8 4
   ───
     0      ③ Subtract.
```

( 2 )

```
32 ) 9 6
```

( 3 )

```
34 ) 6 8
```

( 4 )

```
44 ) 8 8
```

( 5 )

```
36 ) 7 2
```

( 6 )

```
26 ) 7 8
```

**2** Rewrite the problem vertically. Then divide.

( 1 ) 6 9 ÷ 2 3

( 2 ) 7 6 ÷ 3 8

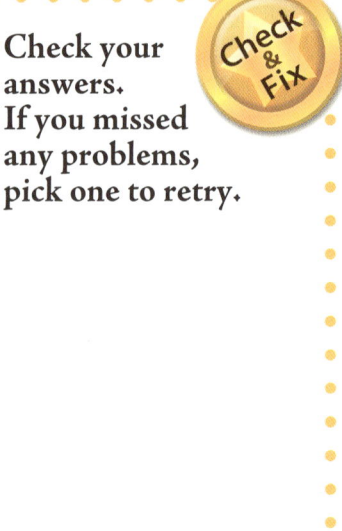

Check your answers. If you missed any problems, pick one to retry.

82

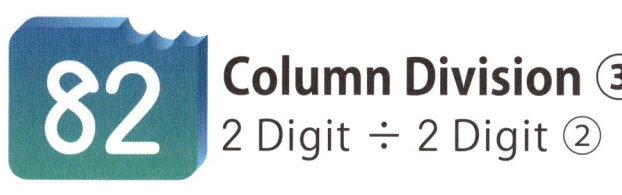

## Column Division ③
### 2 Digit ÷ 2 Digit ②

**1** Divide.

(1)

```
        4 R 2
21 ) 8 6
     8 4
       2
```

(3)

```
32 ) 9 7
```

(5)

```
45 ) 9 2
```

(2)

```
23 ) 4 9
```

(4)

```
24 ) 7 5
```

(6)

```
23 ) 9 7
```

**2** Rewrite the problem vertically. Then divide.

(1) 9 5 ÷ 3 1

(2) 5 4 ÷ 2 5

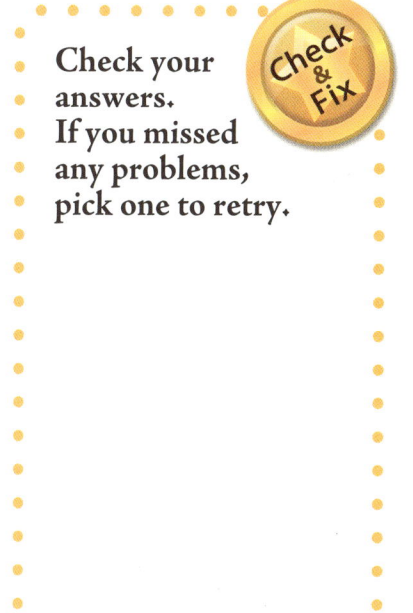

Check your answers. If you missed any problems, pick one to retry.

Check & Fix

# 83 Column Division ③
## 2 Digit ÷ 2 Digit ③

Name

Date / /

Score / 6

**1** Divide.

(1)

```
      3 R 4
12 ) 4 0
      3 6
        4
```

① You can try estimating as 40÷10=4.

```
      4
12 ) 4 0
    4 8  ← ② It cannot be subtracted.
```

③ 4 is must be too large, so reduce it by 1.

```
      3
12 ) 4 0
      3 6
        4
```

(2)

```
23 ) 6 2
```

(3)

```
14 ) 5 8
```

(4)

```
24 ) 8 9
```

**2** Rewrite the problem vertically. Then divide.

(1) 54 ÷ 12

(2) 68 ÷ 24

Check your answers. If you missed any problems, pick one to retry.

Check & Fix

Name

Date    /    /

Score    / 6

**1** Divide.

(1)

$$27 \overline{)82}$$    3 R 1

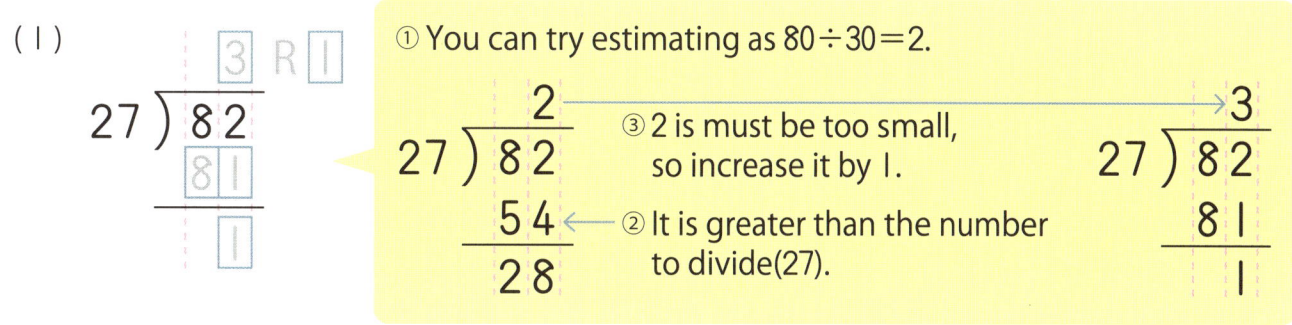

① You can try estimating as 80÷30＝2.

$$27 \overline{)\begin{array}{r} 2 \\ 82 \\ 54 \\ \hline 28 \end{array}}$$

③ 2 is must be too small, so increase it by 1.

② It is greater than the number to divide(27).

$$27 \overline{)\begin{array}{r} 3 \\ 82 \\ 81 \\ \hline 1 \end{array}}$$

(2)

$$37 \overline{)74}$$

(3)

$$16 \overline{)65}$$

(4)

$$17 \overline{)86}$$

**2** Rewrite the problem vertically. Then divide.

(1) 68 ÷ 17

(2) 73 ÷ 36

Check your answers. If you missed any problems, pick one to retry.

Check & Fix

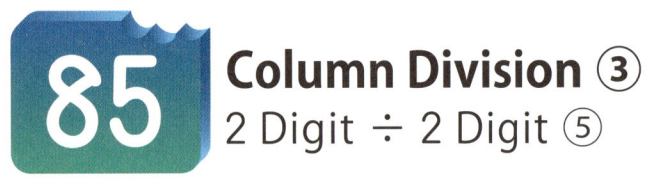

**Column Division ③**

2 Digit ÷ 2 Digit ⑤

Name

Date / /

Score / 6

**1** Divide.

(1)

$$21\overline{)63}$$

(2)

$$32\overline{)98}$$

(3)

$$23\overline{)87}$$

**2** Rewrite the problem vertically. Then divide.

(1) $65 \div 21$

(2) $80 \div 26$

**3** Jaden studied 93 hours over 31 days. If he studied the same number of hours each day, how many hours did he study each day?

Check your answers. If you missed any problems, pick one to retry.

Check & Fix

Ans. _____ hours

86

# 86 Column Division ③
## 2 Digit ÷ 2 Digit ⑥

**1** Divide.

(1)

$$22 \overline{)44}$$

(2)

$$24 \overline{)58}$$

(3)

$$18 \overline{)74}$$

**2** Rewrite the problem vertically. Then divide.

(1) $73 \div 24$

(2) $42 \div 13$

**3** Sally has 76 dog treats. She wants to feed the same amount to each of the 24 dogs at the shelter. How many treats will each dog get? How many will be leftover?

Check your answers. If you missed any problems, pick one to retry.

Ans. _____ treats, _____ remain(s)

Name

Date          /          /

Score

    / 6

**1** Divide.

( 1 )

$14\overline{)28}$

( 2 )

$25\overline{)53}$

( 3 )

$17\overline{)88}$

**2** Rewrite the problem vertically. Then divide.

( 1 )  48 ÷ 12

( 2 )  75 ÷ 13

**3** June makes 86 chocolates for a bake sale. If she places 12 chocolates in a bag, how many bags can she make and how many pieces will be leftover?

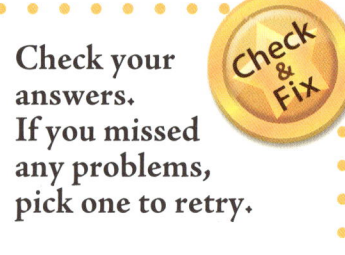

Check your answers. If you missed any problems, pick one to retry.

Ans.          bags,          pieces remain(s)

**Mental Arithmetic ③**
3 Digit ÷ 2 Digit ①

Name

Date   /   /

Score   / 11

**1** Divide.

(1) $120 \div 30 =$

(2) $200 \div 40 =$

(3) $140 \div 20 =$

(4) $560 \div 70 =$

(5) $360 \div 60 =$

(6) $200 \div 40 =$

(7) $100 \div 50 =$

(8) $270 \div 30 =$

(9) $630 \div 90 =$

(10) $160 \div 80 =$

**2** Miles has 480 feet of rope. He wants to cut the rope into pieces that are 60 feet long. How many pieces will he have?

Ans. _____ pieces

Check your answers.
If you missed any
problems, pick one
to retry.

Name

Date      /      /

Score      / 11

**I** Divide.

(1) $160 \div 30 =$

(6) $170 \div 20 =$

(2) $260 \div 50 =$

(7) $580 \div 60 =$

(3) $690 \div 90 =$

(8) $300 \div 40 =$

(4) $430 \div 80 =$

(9) $660 \div 70 =$

(5) $350 \div 40 =$

(10) $400 \div 60 =$

**2** Mrs. Lane has 380 sheets of paper. She wants to divide them into stacks of 50. How many stacks can she make and how many sheets of paper will be leftover?

Ans.            stacks,            sheet(s) remain(s)

Check your answers.
If you missed any
problems, pick one
to retry.

**1** Divide.

( 1 )

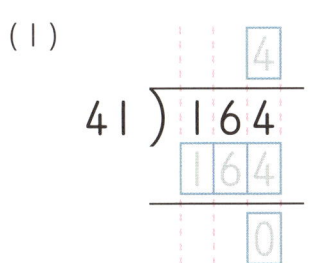

$$41 \overline{)164}$$

( 2 )

$$72 \overline{)374}$$

( 3 )

$$74 \overline{)450}$$

**2** Rewrite the problem vertically. Then divide.

( 1 ) 100 ÷ 25

( 2 ) 154 ÷ 52

**3** Mrs. Smith has 240 sheets of colored paper. If she divides the sheets evenly between her 25 students, how many sheets will each student get and how many will be leftover?

Check your answers. If you missed any problems, pick one to retry.

Check & Fix

Ans. _____ sheets per student, _____ sheet(s) remain(s)

91

# 91 Column Division ④
## 3 Digit ÷ 2 Digit ②

**1** Divide.

(1)

$$\begin{array}{r} 1\ 7\ \text{R}\ 1\ 2 \\ 21\overline{)369} \\ 21\downarrow \\ \hline 1\ 5\ 9 \\ 1\ 4\ 7 \\ \hline 1\ 2 \end{array}$$

(3)

$$32\overline{)679}$$

(5)

$$16\overline{)702}$$

(2)

$$47\overline{)564}$$

(4)

$$18\overline{)648}$$

(6)

$$35\overline{)900}$$

**2** Rewrite the problem vertically. Then divide.

(1) $824 \div 37$

(2) $852 \div 15$

Check your answers. If you missed any problems, pick one to retry.

**92** **Column Division** ④
3 Digit ÷ 2 Digit ③

Name

Date / /

Score / 8

**1** Divide.

(1)
```
        40 R 12
21 ) 852
     84↓
       12
```

(3)
```
18 ) 547
```

(5)
```
13 ) 780
```

(2)
```
46 ) 950
```

(4)
```
35 ) 704
```

(6)
```
16 ) 640
```

**2** Rewrite the problem vertically. Then divide.

(1) 945 ÷ 31

(2) 730 ÷ 18

Check your answers.
If you missed any problems, pick one to retry.

Check & Fix

# 93 Column Division ④
## 3 Digit ÷ 2 Digit ④

**1** Divide.

( 1 )

$$63 \overline{)191}$$

( 2 )

$$42 \overline{)304}$$

( 3 )

$$24 \overline{)230}$$

**2** Rewrite the problem vertically. Then divide.

( 1 ) $324 \div 84$

( 2 ) $651 \div 32$

**3** A florist is making bouquets. He has 195 flowers and wants to place 32 flowers in each bouquet. How many bouquets can he make and how many flowers will be leftover?

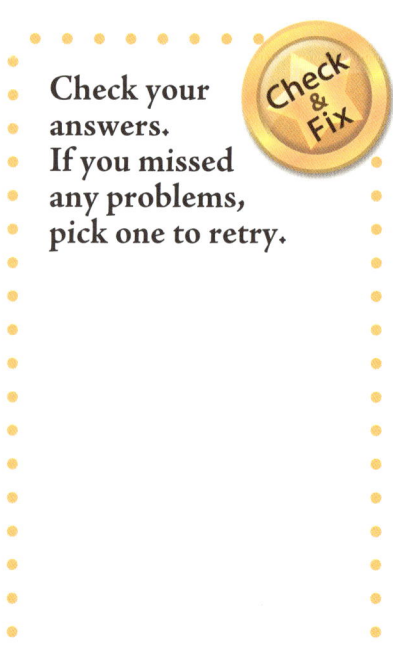

Check your answers. If you missed any problems, pick one to retry.

Ans. _____ bouquets, _____ flower(s) remain(s)

## Column Division ④
### 3 Digit ÷ 2 Digit ⑤

**1** Divide.

(1)

$$53 \overline{)243}$$

(2)

$$33 \overline{)304}$$

(3)

$$24 \overline{)296}$$

**2** Rewrite the problem vertically. Then divide.

(1) $416 \div 53$

(2) $487 \div 64$

**3** Luke has 900 peanuts. He wants to divide them into bags of 35 for a baseball team. How many bags can he make and how many peanuts will be leftover?

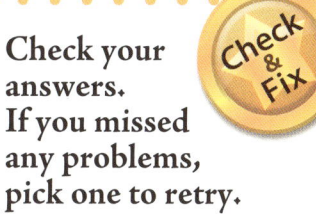

Check your answers. If you missed any problems, pick one to retry.

Ans.            bags,            peanut(s) remain(s)

Name

Date / /

Score / 6

**1** Divide.

(1)

81 ) 633

(2)

32 ) 121

(3)

24 ) 480

**2** Rewrite the problem vertically. Then divide.

(1) 172 ÷ 34

(2) 362 ÷ 49

**3** There are 480 students going on a field trip. Each bus can take 24 students. How many buses are needed?

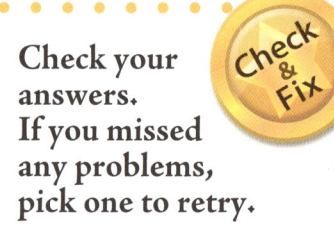

Check your answers. If you missed any problems, pick one to retry.

Ans.                buses

# 96 Final Practice
## Mental Arithmetic

**1** Divide.

(1)  $8 \div 2 =$

(2)  $25 \div 4 =$

(3)  $40 \div 20 =$

(4)  $30 \div 10 =$

(5)  $60 \div 2 =$

(6)  $34 \div 9 =$

(7)  $90 \div 80 =$

(8)  $42 \div 7 =$

(9)  $210 \div 30 =$

(10)  $170 \div 50 =$

**2** Erin made 27 bracelets. She divided them equally among her 4 friends. How many bracelets did each friend get and how many were leftover for Erin?

Ans.          bracelets,          remain(s)

**Check your answers. If you missed any problems, pick one to retry.**

97

# Final Practice
## 2 Digit ÷ 1 Digit

Name

Date / /

Score / 6

**1** Divide.

( 1 )

$$3 \overline{)51}$$

( 2 )

$$7 \overline{)56}$$

( 3 )

$$3 \overline{)64}$$

**2** Rewrite the problem vertically. Then divide.

( 1 ) $48 \div 4$

( 2 ) $35 \div 2$

**3** Mika's mom gave her $68 to share with her sister. If she splits the money equally with her sister, how much will they each get?

Ans. $ _____

**Final Practice**
3 Digit ÷ 1 Digit

**1** Divide.

( 1 )

$$2 \overline{)563}$$

( 2 )

$$6 \overline{)245}$$

( 3 )

$$4 \overline{)820}$$

**2** Rewrite the problem vertically. Then divide.

( 1 ) $208 \div 4$

( 2 ) $848 \div 4$

**3** 534 people attended a concert over 2 days. If the same number of people went each night, how many people saw the concert each night?

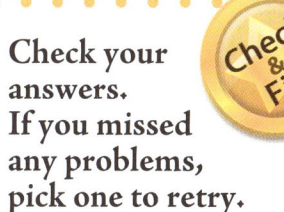

Check your answers. If you missed any problems, pick one to retry.

Ans. _____ people

## Final Practice
### 2 Digit ÷ 2 Digit

Name

Date
/ /

Score
/ 6

**1** Divide.

( 1 )

24 ) 76

( 2 )

31 ) 93

( 3 )

18 ) 91

**2** Rewrite the problem vertically. Then divide.

( 1 ) 86 ÷ 12

( 2 ) 72 ÷ 21

**3** Hannah's chickens laid 92 eggs this week. She makes cartons with 18 eggs in each. How many cartons can she make? Will she have any eggs left over?

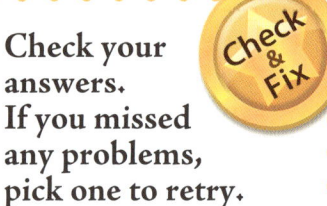

Check your answers. If you missed any problems, pick one to retry.

Ans.            cartons,            egg(s) remain(s)

# Final Practice

3 Digit ÷ 2 Digit

**1** Divide.

(1)

62) 369

(2)

40) 250

(3)

17) 187

**2** Rewrite the problem vertically. Then divide.

(1) 640 ÷ 32

(2) 195 ÷ 32

**3** Dana made 296 chocolates for her classmates. If she divides the chocolates evenly among her 24 classmates, how many chocolates will each classmate get and how many will be leftover?

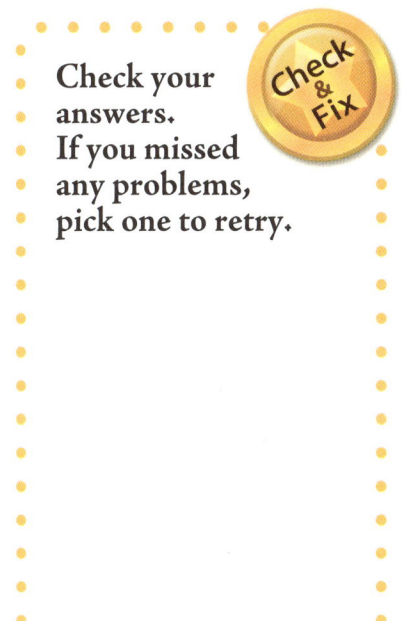

Check your answers. If you missed any problems, pick one to retry.

Ans. _____ chocolates, _____ remain(s)

# MathBites
## Multiplication & Division Grade 4
# Answer Key

**1** Mental Arithmetic
2× through 5× p.2

**1** (1)2 (3)14 (5)24 (7)20 (9)15

(2)6 (4)12 (6)8 (8)36 (10)30

**2** 3×7＝21　Ans. $21

**2** Mental Arithmetic
6× through 9× and 1× p.3

**1** (1)12 (3)7 (5)24 (7)36 (9)6

(2)48 (4)35 (6)56 (8)81 (10)8

**2** 8×6＝48　Ans. 48 peaches

**3** Mental Arithmetic
×10 through ×12 p.4

**1** (1)10 (3)40 (5)90 (7)66 (9)12

(2)20 (4)70 (6)33 (8)88 (10)60

**2** 5×11＝55　Ans. 55 apples

**4** Mental Arithmetic
10× through 12× , 0× and ×0 p.5

**1** (1)10 (3)22 (5)12 (7)0 (9)0

(2)30 (4)66 (6)60 (8)0 (10)0

**2** 12×4＝48　Ans. 48 eggs

**5** Mental Arithmetic
Multiplication of Tens and Hundreds p.6

**1** (1)60 (3)450 (5)720 (7)200 (9)4900

(2)150 (4)120 (6)600 (8)800 (10)3200

**2** 60×3＝180　Ans. 180 cards

**6** Mental Arithmetic
Mixed ① p.7

**1** (1)6 (3)40 (5)33 (7)24 (9)120

(2)45 (4)7 (6)70 (8)0 (10)2400

**2** 9×5＝45　Ans. 45 students

**7** Mental Arithmetic
Mixed ② p.8

**1** (1)28 (3)18 (5)50 (7)50 (9)90

(2)12 (4)56 (6)12 (8)0 (10)2700

**2** 20×8＝160　Ans. $160

**8** Column Multiplication ①
2 Digit × 1 Digit ① p.9

**1** (1)36 (2)93 (3)84

**2** (1)88 (2)88

**3** 12×4＝48　Ans. 48 cans

**9** **Column Multiplication ①**
**2 Digit × 1 Digit ②** p.10

**1** (1) 72  (2) 81  (3) 90

**2** (1) 87  (2) 80

**3** 24 × 4 = 96    Ans. 96 strawberries

**10** **Column Multiplication ①**
**2 Digit × 1 Digit ③** p.11

**1** (1) 128  (2) 128  (3) 249

**2** (1) 168  (2) 208

**3** 62 × 4 = 248    Ans. 248 students

**11** **Column Multiplication ①**
**2 Digit × 1 Digit ④** p.12

**1** (1) 80  (2) 300  (3) 210

**2** (1) 540  (2) 90

**3** 60 × 4 = 240    Ans. 240 miles

**12** **Column Multiplication ①**
**2 Digit × 1 Digit ⑤** p.13

**1** (1) 228  (2) 144  (3) 432

**2** (1) 448  (2) 230

**3** 25 × 6 = 150    Ans. $150

**13** **Column Multiplication ①**
**2 Digit × 1 Digit ⑥** p.14

**1** (1) 111  (2) 128  (3) 100

**2** (1) 116  (2) 117

**3** 35 × 3 = 105    Ans. 105 buttons

**14** **Column Multiplication ①**
**2 Digit × 1 Digit ⑦** p.15

**1** (1) 207  (2) 504  (3) 308

**2** (1) 342  (2) 609

**3** 24 × 9 = 216    Ans. 216 desks

**15** **Column Multiplication ①**
**2 Digit × 1 Digit ⑧** p.16

**1** (1) 84  (2) 328  (3) 477

**2** (1) 400  (2) 216

**3** 16 × 7 = 112    Ans. 112 cars

**16** **Column Multiplication ①**
**2 Digit × 1 Digit ⑨** p.17

**1** (1) 78  (2) 480  (3) 228

**2** (1) 86  (2) 102

**3** 75 × 8 = 600    Ans. $600

**17** **Column Multiplication ②**
**3 Digit × 1 Digit ①** p.18

**1** (1) 628  (3) 842  (5) 963

　　(2) 396  (4) 484  (6) 488

**2** (1) 699  (2) 826

**18** **Column Multiplication ②**
**3 Digit × 1 Digit ②** p.19

**1** (1) 696  (3) 945  (5) 850

　　(2) 864  (4) 492  (6) 981

**2** (1) 590  (2) 494

**19** **Column Multiplication ②**
3 **Digit** × 1 **Digit** ③ p.20

**1** (1) 849  (3) 648  (5) 905

(2) 982  (4) 748  (6) 726

**2** (1) 728  (2) 926

**20** **Column Multiplication ②**
3 **Digit** × 1 **Digit** ④ p.21

**1** (1) 734  (2) 785  (3) 952

**2** (1) 680  (2) 822

**3** 145 × 6 = 870   Ans. $870

**21** **Column Multiplication ②**
3 **Digit** × 1 **Digit** ⑤ p.22

**1** (1) 512  (3) 826  (5) 500

(2) 705  (4) 812  (6) 711

**2** (1) 904  (2) 714

**22** **Column Multiplication ②**
3 **Digit** × 1 **Digit** ⑥ p.23

**1** (1) 960  (3) 800  (5) 600

(2) 860  (4) 810  (6) 760

**2** (1) 900  (2) 920

**23** **Column Multiplication ②**
3 **Digit** × 1 **Digit** ⑦ p.24

**1** (1) 432  (3) 615  (5) 530

(2) 814  (4) 608  (6) 836

**2** (1) 918  (2) 820

**24** **Column Multiplication ②**
3 **Digit** × 1 **Digit** ⑧ p.25

**1** (1) 1284  (2) 1286  (3) 2055

**2** (1) 1839  (2) 1884

**3** 521 × 4 = 2,084   Ans. 2,084 staples

**25** **Column Multiplication ②**
3 **Digit** × 1 **Digit** ⑨ p.26

**1** (1) 1272  (3) 1290  (5) 3070

(2) 1281  (4) 1472  (6) 1587

**2** (1) 2448  (2) 2090

**26** **Column Multiplication ②**
3 **Digit** × 1 **Digit** ⑩ p.27

**1** (1) 1528  (3) 2706  (5) 1748

(2) 1959  (4) 1305  (6) 2768

**2** (1) 1446  (2) 3205

**27** **Column Multiplication ②**
3 **Digit** × 1 **Digit** ⑪ p.28

**1** (1) 1548  (3) 4470  (5) 2340

(2) 4564  (4) 7767  (6) 4768

**2** (1) 1434  (2) 2380

**28** **Column Multiplication ②**
3 **Digit** × 1 **Digit** ⑫ p.29

**1** (1) 1164  (2) 1296  (3) 1056

**2** (1) 1188  (2) 1140

**3** 364 × 3 = 1,092   Ans. 1,092 cards

**29** Column Multiplication ②
3 Digit × 1 Digit ⑬ p.30

1 (1) 1611 (3) 2904 (5) 3300

(2) 2514 (4) 2226 (6) 4112

2 (1) 2516 (2) 2505

**30** Column Multiplication ②
3 Digit × 1 Digit ⑭ p.31

1 (1) 3168 (3) 2286 (5) 4067

(2) 2019 (4) 2008 (6) 3048

2 (1) 2076 (2) 4149

**31** Column Multiplication ②
3 Digit × 1 Digit ⑮ p.32

1 (1) 2334 (3) 3100 (5) 3402

(2) 5112 (4) 4122 (6) 5004

2 (1) 2104 (2) 3116

**32** Column Multiplication ②
3 Digit × 1 Digit ⑯ p.33

1 (1) 1360 (2) 3521 (3) 5200

2 (1) 3420 (2) 2030

3 850 × 4 = 3,400 Ans. 3,400 people

**33** Column Multiplication ②
3 Digit × 1 Digit ⑰ p.34

1 (1) 372 (2) 2469 (3) 1296

2 (1) 879 (2) 2928

3 486 × 2 = 972 Ans. 972 inches

**34** Column Multiplication ②
3 Digit × 1 Digit ⑱ p.35

1 (1) 888 (2) 816 (3) 1875

2 (1) 488 (2) 6006

3 625 × 3 = 1,875 Ans. 1,875 grams

**35** Column Multiplication ③
2 Digit × 2 Digit ① p.36

1 (1) 882 (3) 288 (5) 594

(2) 992 (4) 299 (6) 672

2 (1) 294 (2) 396

**36** Column Multiplication ③
2 Digit × 2 Digit ② p.37

1 (1) 984 (3) 360 (5) 792

(2) 882 (4) 798 (6) 882

2 (1) 864 (2) 930

**37** Column Multiplication ③
2 Digit × 2 Digit ③ p.38

**1** (1)736 (3)836 (5)935

(2)504 (4)510 (6)504

**2** (1)903 (2)444

**38** Column Multiplication ③
2 Digit × 2 Digit ④ p.39

**1** (1)896 (2)624 (3)490

**2** (1)648 (2)504

**3** 25 × 24 = 600    Ans. 600 ice pops

**39** Column Multiplication ③
2 Digit × 2 Digit ⑤ p.40

**1** (1)1175 (3)1104 (5)1014

(2)1036 (4)1092 (6)1170

**2** (1)1152 (2)1053

**40** Column Multiplication ③
2 Digit × 2 Digit ⑥ p.41

**1** (1)1476 (3)1886 (5)3266

(2)1431 (4)1470 (6)2108

**2** (1)1992 (2)1504

**41** Column Multiplication ③
2 Digit × 2 Digit ⑦ p.42

**1** (1)1944 (3)1620 (5)2006

(2)2814 (4)5312 (6)3120

**2** (1)1288 (2)4484

**42** Column Multiplication ③
2 Digit × 2 Digit ⑧ p.43

**1** (1)1680 (2)850 (3)1400

**2** (1)3480 (2)5200

**3** 60 × 34 = 2,040    Ans. 2,040 seeds

**43** Column Multiplication ③
2 Digit × 2 Digit ⑨ p.44

**1** (1)630 (2)980 (3)4380

**2** (1)5360 (2)2700

**3** 24 × 30 = 720    Ans. 720 desks

**44** Column Multiplication ③
2 Digit × 2 Digit ⑩ p.45

**1** (1)576 (2)1512 (3)1026

**2** (1)800 (2)4480

**3** 32 × 21 = 672    Ans. 672 straws

**45** **Column Multiplication ③**
**2 Digit × 2 Digit ⑪ p.46**

**1** (1) 288　(2) 989　(3) 2880

**2** (1) 1008　(2) 1955

**3** 23 × 28 = 644　　Ans. 644 toy cars


**46** **Column Multiplication ③**
**2 Digit × 2 Digit ⑫ p.47**

**1** (1) 816　(2) 2208　(3) 1400

**2** (1) 850　(2) 384

**3** 70 × 45 = 3,150　　Ans. 3,150 seeds


**47** **Final Practice**
**Mental Arithmetic p.48**

**1** (1) 18　(3) 42　(5) 30　(7) 12　(9) 700

　　(2) 30　(4) 8　(6) 44　(8) 0　(10) 240

**2** 7 × 4 = 28　　Ans. $28


**48** **Final Practice**
**2 Digit × 1 Digit p.49**

**1** (1) 84　(2) 200　(3) 406

**2** (1) 99　(2) 188

**3** 26 × 4 = 104　　Ans. 104 sunflowers


**49** **Final Practice**
**3 Digit × 1 Digit p.50**

**1** (1) 309　(2) 876　(3) 1086

**2** (1) 904　(2) 1230

**3** 514 × 8 = 4,112　　Ans. 4,112 crayons


**50** **Final Practice**
**2 Digit × 2 Digit p.51**

**1** (1) 1536　(2) 2560　(3) 528

**2** (1) 384　(2) 4140

**3** 14 × 36 = 504　　Ans. 504 sheets


**51** **Mental Arithmetic ①**
**÷ 2 through ÷ 5 p.52**

**1** (1) 4　(3) 8　(5) 7　(7) 5　(9) 3

　　(2) 6　(4) 2　(6) 1　(8) 9　(10) 8

**2** 12 ÷ 3 = 4　　Ans. 4 bananas


**52** **Mental Arithmetic ①**
**÷ 6 through ÷ 10, ÷ 1, and 0 ÷ p.53**

**1** (1) 3　(3) 4　(5) 5　(7) 2　(9) 9

　　(2) 8　(4) 7　(6) 1　(8) 6　(10) 0

**2** 72 ÷ 8 = 9　　Ans. 9 gumballs


**53** **Mental Arithmetic ①**
**÷ 2 through ÷ 5 with Remeinders p.54**

**1** (1) 2 R1　(4) 2 R2　(7) 4 R3　(10) 7 R4

　　(2) 3 R1　(5) 8 R1　(8) 9 R2

　　(3) 6 R1　(6) 1 R2　(9) 4 R3

**2** 25 ÷ 3 = 8 R1　　Ans. 8 carrots, 1 remains


**54** **Mental Arithmetic ①**
**÷ 6 through ÷ 9 with Remeinders p.55**

**1** (1) 2 R2　(4) 1 R1　(7) 4 R1　(10) 8 R6

　　(2) 2 R5　(5) 8 R3　(8) 8 R5

　　(3) 7 R4　(6) 2 R4　(9) 3 R4

**2** 45 ÷ 6 = 7 R3　　Ans. 7 cookies, 3 remain

**55** Mental Arithmetic ① Division of Tens p.56

**1** (1) 10 (3) 10 (5) 20 (7) 40 (9) 10

 (2) 10 (4) 20 (6) 30 (8) 30 (10) 20

**2** 60 ÷ 3 = 20    Ans. 20 books

**56** Mental Arithmetic ① Mixed ① p.57

**1** (1) 2 (3) 5 (5) 2 R1 (7) 2 R3 (9) 3 R7

 (2) 7 (4) 9 (6) 4 R3 (8) 8 R6 (10) 40

**2** 14 ÷ 2 = 7    Ans. 7 books

**57** Mental Arithmetic ① Mixed ② p.58

**1** (1) 8 (3) 7 (5) 3 R1 (7) 6 R1 (9) 1 R2

 (2) 4 (4) 6 (6) 7 R3 (8) 5 R2 (10) 10

**2** 36 ÷ 4 = 9    Ans. 9 cupcakes

**58** Mental Arithmetic ① Mixed ③ p.59

**1** (1) 4 (3) 8 (5) 6 R1 (7) 2 R1 (9) 3 R5

 (2) 4 (4) 0 (6) 7 R2 (8) 9 R5 (10) 20

**2** 72 ÷ 9 = 8    Ans. 8 pages

**59** Column Division ① 2 Digit ÷ 1 Digit ① p.60

**1** (1) 6 R2 (2) 7 R4 (3) 9 R1

**2** (1) 5 (2) 8 R2

**3** 42 ÷ 6 = 7    Ans. 7 boxes

**60** Column Division ① 2 Digit ÷ 1 Digit ② p.61

**1** (1) 23 (2) 23 (3) 21

**2** (1) 41 (2) 11

**3** 63 ÷ 3 = 21    Ans. 21 kids

**61** Column Division ① 2 Digit ÷ 1 Digit ③ p.62

**1** (1) 19 (2) 25 (3) 13

**2** (1) 38 (2) 23

**3** 75 ÷ 5 = 15    Ans. 15 lollipops

**62** Column Division ① 2 Digit ÷ 1 Digit ④ p.63

**1** (1) 22 R1 (2) 32 R1 (3) 32 R2

**2** (1) 11 R3 (2) 24 R1

**3** 64 ÷ 3 = 21 R1    Ans. 21 potatoes, 1 remains

**63** Column Division ① 2 Digit ÷ 1 Digit ⑤ p.64

**1** (1) 15 R1 (2) 16 R2 (3) 35 R1

**2** (1) 17 R2 (2) 28 R1

**3** 84 ÷ 5 = 16 R4    Ans. 16 pieces, 4 cm remain

**64** Column Division ① 2 Digit ÷ 1 Digit ⑥ p.65

**1** (1) 20 R3 (2) 10 R5 (3) 40 R1

**2** (1) 30 (2) 10 R2

**3** 82 ÷ 4 = 20 R2

Ans. 20 pieces, 2 inches remain

**65** **Column Division ①**
2 **Digit ÷ I Digit** ⑦ p.66

**1** (1) 5 R3  (2) 14  (3) 30 R I

**2** (1) 34  (2) 12 R6

**3** 56 ÷ 7 = 8  Ans. 8 teams


**66** **Column Division ①**
2 **Digit ÷ I Digit** ⑧ p.67

**1** (1) 3 R7  (2) 31  (3) 16 R4

**2** (1) 29  (2) 32 R I

**3** 93 ÷ 3 = 31  Ans. 31 classmates


**67** **Column Division ①**
2 **Digit ÷ I Digit** ⑨ p.68

**1** (1) 21 R2  (2) 24 R3  (3) 10

**2** (1) 3 R2  (2) 15

**3** 92 ÷ 3 = 30 R2  Ans. 30 carts, 2 remain


**68** **Column Division ②**
3 **Digit ÷ I Digit** ① p.69

**1** (1) 231  (3) 221  (5) 323

(2) 314  (4) 224

**2** (1) 131  (2) 332


**69** **Column Division ②**
3 **Digit ÷ I Digit** ② p.70

**1** (1) 252  (3) 137  (5) 156

(2) 218  (4) 296

**2** (1) 157  (2) 224


**70** **Column Division ②**
3 **Digit ÷ I Digit** ③ p.71

**1** (1) 163 R2  (3) 123 R2  (5) 123 R2

(2) 435 R I  (4) 227 R I

**2** (1) 312 R2  (2) 176 R3


**71** **Column Division ②**
3 **Digit ÷ I Digit** ④ p.72

**1** (1) 210 R3  (2) 470  (3) 130 R5

**2** (1) 180 R I  (2) 120

**3** 845 ÷ 6 = 140 R5

Ans. 140 glasses, 5 oz remain


**72** **Column Division ②**
3 **Digit ÷ I Digit** ⑤ p.73

**1** (1) 208  (3) 104 R I  (5) 300 R2

(2) 402 R I  (4) 207 R2  (6) 308 R I

**2** (1) 203  (2) 103 R4

**73** **Column Division** ② 
**3 Digit ÷ 1 Digit** ⑥ p.74

**1** (1) 71 (3) 52 (5) 61

(2) 61 R2 (4) 91 R1 (6) 91 R1

**2** (1) 72 R2 (2) 34

**74** **Column Division** ② 
**3 Digit ÷ 1 Digit** ⑦ p.75

**1** (1) 69 (3) 84 (5) 62 R4

(2) 56 R1 (4) 64 (6) 14 R2

**2** (1) 76 R2 (2) 75

**75** **Column Division** ② 
**3 Digit ÷ 1 Digit** ⑧ p.76

**1** (1) 80 R2 (2) 60 (3) 70

**2** (1) 70 R4 (2) 90

**3** 180 ÷ 6 = 30    Ans. 30 crates

**76** **Column Division** ② 
**3 Digit ÷ 1 Digit** ⑨ p.77

**1** (1) 267 (2) 130 R4 (3) 82 R1

**2** (1) 222 (2) 50 R4

**3** 462 ÷ 2 = 231    Ans. 231 inches

**77** **Column Division** ② 
**3 Digit ÷ 1 Digit** ⑩ p.78

**1** (1) 123 (2) 123 R5 (3) 20 R5

**2** (1) 231 (2) 103 R1

**3** 743 ÷ 3 = 247 R2

Ans. 247 yards, 2 remain

**78** **Column Division** ② 
**3 Digit ÷ 1 Digit** ⑪ p.79

**1** (1) 215 (2) 160 R2 (3) 64 R3

**2** (1) 248 R1 (2) 206 R1

**3** 128 ÷ 9 = 14 R2

Ans. 14 colored pencils, 2 remain

**79** **Mental Arithmetic** ② 
**2 Digit ÷ 2 Digit** ① p.80

**1** (1) 2 (3) 2 (5) 3 (7) 5 (9) 2

(2) 3 (4) 3 (6) 2 (8) 7 (10) 4

**2** 60 ÷ 20 = 3    Ans. 3 pieces

**80** **Mental Arithmetic** ② 
**2 Digit ÷ 2 Digit** ② p.81

**1** (1) 1 R10 (4) 3 R10 (7) 2 R10 (10) 1 R30

(2) 2 R10 (5) 2 R10 (8) 2 R20

(3) 1 R20 (6) 1 R20 (9) 4 R10

**2** 90 ÷ 40 = 2 R10    Ans. 2 models, $10 remain

**81** Column Division ③
2 Digit ÷ 2 Digit ① p.82

**1** (1) 4 (3) 2 (5) 2

   (2) 3 (4) 2 (6) 3

**2** (1) 3 (2) 2

**82** Column Division ③
2 Digit ÷ 2 Digit ② p.83

**1** (1) 4 R2 (3) 3 R1 (5) 2 R2

   (2) 2 R3 (4) 3 R3 (6) 4 R5

**2** (1) 3 R2 (2) 2 R4

**83** Column Division ③
2 Digit ÷ 2 Digit ③ p.84

**1** (1) 3 R4 (3) 4 R2

   (2) 2 R16 (4) 3 R17

**2** (1) 4 R6 (2) 2 R20

**84** Column Division ③
2 Digit ÷ 2 Digit ④ p.85

**1** (1) 3 R1 (3) 4 R1

   (2) 2 (4) 5 R1

**2** (1) 4 (2) 2 R1

**85** Column Division ③
2 Digit ÷ 2 Digit ⑤ p.86

**1** (1) 3 (2) 3 R2 (3) 3 R18

**2** (1) 3 R2 (2) 3 R2

**3** $93 ÷ 31 = 3$ Ans. 3 hours

**86** Column Division ③
2 Digit ÷ 2 Digit ⑥ p.87

**1** (1) 2 (2) 2 R10 (3) 4 R2

**2** (1) 3 R1 (2) 3 R3

**3** $76 ÷ 24 = 3$ R4 Ans. 3 treats, 4 remain

**87** Column Division ③
2 Digit ÷ 2 Digit ⑦ p.88

**1** (1) 2 (2) 2 R3 (3) 5 R3

**2** (1) 4 (2) 5 R10

**3** $86 ÷ 12 = 7$ R2 Ans. 7 bags, 2 pieces remain

**88** Mental Arithmetic ③
3 Digit ÷ 2 Digit ① p.89

**1** (1) 4 (3) 7 (5) 6 (7) 2 (9) 7

   (2) 5 (4) 8 (6) 5 (8) 9 (10) 2

**2** $480 ÷ 60 = 8$ Ans. 8 pieces

**89** Mental Arithmetic ③
3 Digit ÷ 2 Digit ② p.90

**1** (1) 5 R10 (4) 5 R30 (7) 9 R40 (10) 6 R40

   (2) 5 R10 (5) 8 R30 (8) 7 R20

   (3) 7 R60 (6) 8 R10 (9) 9 R30

**2** $380 ÷ 50 = 7$ R30

                    Ans. 7 stacks, 30 sheets remain

**90** Column Division ④
3 Digit ÷ 2 Digit ① p.91

**1** (1) 4 (2) 5 R14 (3) 6 R6

**2** (1) 4 (2) 2 R50

**3** $240 ÷ 25 = 9$ R15

    Ans. 9 sheets per student, 15 sheets remain

**91** **Column Division ④**
**3 Digit ÷ 2 Digit ② p.92**

1 (1) 17 R12 (3) 21 R7 (5) 43 R14

(2) 12 (4) 36 (6) 25 R25

2 (1) 22 R10 (2) 56 R12

**92** **Column Division ④**
**3 Digit ÷ 2 Digit ③ p.93**

1 (1) 40 R12 (3) 30 R7 (5) 60

(2) 20 R30 (4) 20 R4 (6) 40

2 (1) 30 R15 (2) 40 R10

**93** **Column Division ④**
**3 Digit ÷ 2 Digit ④ p.94**

1 (1) 3 R2 (2) 7 R10 (3) 9 R14

2 (1) 3 R72 (2) 20 R11

3 $195 ÷ 32 = 6$ R3

Ans. 6 bouquets, 3 flowers remain

**94** **Column Division ④**
**3 Digit ÷ 2 Digit ⑤ p.95**

1 (1) 4 R31 (2) 9 R7 (3) 12 R8

2 (1) 7 R45 (2) 7 R39

3 $900 ÷ 35 = 25$ R25

Ans. 25 bags, 25 peanuts remain

**95** **Column Division ④**
**3 Digit ÷ 2 Digit ⑥ p.96**

1 (1) 7 R66 (2) 3 R25 (3) 20

2 (1) 5 R2 (2) 7 R19

3 $480 ÷ 24 = 20$ Ans. 20 buses

**96** **Final Practice**
**Mental Arithmetic p.97**

1 (1) 4 (3) 2 (5) 30 (7) 1 R10 (9) 7

(2) 6 R1 (4) 3 (6) 3 R7 (8) 6 (10) 3 R20

2 $27 ÷ 4 = 6$ R3 Ans. 6 bracelets, 3 remain

**97** **Final Practice**
**2 Digit ÷ 1 Digit p.98**

1 (1) 17 (2) 8 (3) 21 R1

2 (1) 12 (2) 17 R1

3 $68 ÷ 2 = 34$ Ans. $34

**98** **Final Practice**
**3 Digit ÷ 1 Digit p.99**

1 (1) 281 R1 (2) 40 R5 (3) 205

2 (1) 52 (2) 212

3 $534 ÷ 2 = 267$ Ans. 267 people

**99** **Final Practice**
**2 Digit ÷ 2 Digit p.100**

1 (1) 3 R4 (2) 3 (3) 5 R1

2 (1) 7 R2 (2) 3 R9

3 $92 ÷ 18 = 5$ R2

Ans. 5 cartons, 2 eggs remain

**100** **Final Practice**
**3 Digit ÷ 2 Digit p.101**

1 (1) 5 R59 (2) 6 R10 (3) 11

2 (1) 20 (2) 6 R3

3 $296 ÷ 24 = 12$ R8

Ans. 12 chocolates, 8 remain